COLLEGES AND COMMITMENTS

COLLEGES
AND
COMMITMENTS

Edited by
Lloyd J. Averill and William W. Jellema

THE WESTMINSTER PRESS
Philadelphia

370.1
Av3c
76661
nov. 1971

Copyright © MCMLXXI The Westminster Press

ISBN 0–664–24928–0
LIBRARY OF CONGRESS CATALOG CARD No. 70–155900

BOOK DESIGN BY DOROTHY ALDEN SMITH

Published by The Westminster Press
Philadelphia, Pennsylvania ®

PRINTED IN THE UNITED STATES OF AMERICA

To
M. Eugene Osterhaven
and
Weimer K. Hicks
who live out the meaning
of commitment
in higher education

Contents

Part I

THE NATURE AND LEGITIMACY
OF COMMITMENTS

Part II

COMMITMENTS AND THE DIMENSIONS
OF LEARNING

Part III

NORMS AND MODELS OF COMMITMENT

Foreword

IF THE FINANCIAL PLIGHT OF HIGHER EDUCATION IS THE MOST
warmly discussed and debated issue among college administrators and teachers these days, the question of the
value commitments of colleges and universities is surely
not far behind. Nor are the two unrelated. Budgets reflect institutional priorities, which is to say that a college
or university budget is the concrete expression of the institution's commitments. Whether or not public funds can
legitimately be assigned to and accepted by institutions that
give their commitments explicit religious as well as educational form is an issue that will become more rather than
less acute as Congress is pressed to interest itself more and
more in higher education as a matter of national policy.

The issue of institutional commitments is very much
alive in church-related colleges and universities. It has been
made so, in part, by the revival of theological interest that
overtook the intellectual world after World War II. The
question of the relation between faith—in both its intellectual and institutional forms—and culture, which occupies
so large a place in the theological discussion of the last
twenty-five years, comes to pointed focus not only in the
secular city but also in institutions of higher learning.
Roman Catholic preoccupation with the question of commitments in education surely antedates Vatican II but has
been given special impetus by the Council and the events

that have followed. Whether or not laicization means also
secularization is moot. Exigent factors have also forced
the issue upon church-related schools. Competition has
pressed them to face the issue of their identity, and the
possibility of increasing federal funds adds urgency to the
quest.

In 1968 a group of persons "concerned about religiously
committed higher education" met at the invitation of the
University of Notre Dame. Reflecting on that conference,
its chairman, the Reverend James Burtchaell, C.S.C., articu-
lated the uncertainties many educators are voicing:

> Some of us have been asking ourselves whether on any
> long-range view there should be a Notre Dame, or a
> St. Olaf's, or an Iowa Wesleyan, or a Swarthmore. Our
> concern is for the particular way in which some colleges
> and universities are committed to religious development.
> No doubt all colleges, public and private, have some
> fairly clear commitment to values. . . . On certain
> campuses, however, the college itself stands within a
> faith tradition and explicitly undertakes to make reli-
> gious development an eminent feature in the education
> it offers. We could not help asking why this ought really
> be so.
>   . . . The prime guarantee of a college's religious for-
> mation has been control: control of governance, of ad-
> ministration, of teaching and of discipline. As this
> strong control recedes and gives way gradually to spon-
> sorship rather than containment, will an explicitly reli-
> gious commitment endure the wider exposure? In an
> environment where academic competition is accorded
> ultimate preference, can any privilege for religious con-
> viction be retained? If a particular religious tradition

can be understood freely and best within a context of
pluralism, would a purposefully sought openness in the
college population represent reform or disintegration?

Those universities and colleges which intend to face
these uncertainties as stimulating challenges, rather than
threats, need, first of all, an articulate self-understanding.
Those who share in the work should ask how they can
become more flexible yet effective, proud and explicit
rather than bashful or devious about their religious commitment, more aggressive in their critique of an unquestioned American Way of Life.

It was our feeling that with the ground underfoot
shifting so abruptly, many religiously committed colleges
are apprehensive. They are tempted either to throw up
their hands at the relentless pressures of secularization, or
to impose more rigid and less effective restraints upon
ever more restive students. Those to whom these alternatives are unacceptable are being forced back, step
by step, without much vision of what they are backing
into.

Nagging uncertainty and failing vision on issues of institutional commitment are by no means limited to church-
related colleges and universities, however. Curricular innovation is sweeping throughout the higher educational
world, and some teachers and administrators, at least, have
come to see that a college curriculum is "a complex value
judgment," to use the words of Haverford Provost Gerhard
Spiegler. Student activism, if anything more marked on
the public and proudly secular campuses, has forced a reexamination of institutional intent—of the legitimate scope
of institutional concern—by its demand that nonacademic
behavior be excluded from institutional regulation.

Charges that the universities have become the uncritical
servants of the military-industrial complex, and that by
indifferent or unenlightened policies they have exacerbated
the social ills of the communities in which they are set, call
attention to the hidden commitments which may be at
work even where overt commitments are disavowed. The
moot relation between teaching and research, the issue of
open versus selective admission, the problem of racism not
alone in fraternities and sororities but in the curriculum
and in teacher recruitment—all raise urgent questions about
the values educational institutions espouse. If church-related schools are in any different situation from their secular
counterparts, it is only that the problem is, in some ways,
easier for them to acknowledge, since they have a rhetorical
tradition accustomed to talk of commitments, whereas the
secular and public schools have not.

This widespread preoccupation suggests that a volume of
essays dealing forthrightly with the value questions in
higher education would be useful to a reasonably large
reading public. What is offered here is a set of frankly
partisan pieces, or pieces chosen for frankly partisan purposes (as opposed to a more objective and comprehensive
survey), which seem to support the position, from a variety
of locations within higher education and from a variety of
angles of interest, that value commitments are integral,
indispensable, indeed inescapable, in higher education, and
most particularly within the tradition of the liberal arts
and sciences. The purposes of this book, then, are (1) to
give a good conscience to students, teachers, administrators,
trustees, and members of church boards of education who
are trying to insist from their respective places that the
issue of institutional commitments must be faced squarely;
(2) to help them toward additional clarity of thought and
articulation on the issue, in order to avoid as much as

possible what Father Burtchaell described as the process of being forced back, step by step, without much vision of what we are backing into; (3) to suggest some of the forms commitment might legitimately take in the colleges and some of the consequences it might have for the shape of our institutions; and (4) to provide a basic printed resource for wider study, discussion, and debate.

Brief individual introductions are provided for each essay, but it may be useful here to say something about the overall plan of the volume.

Part I treats the nature and legitimacy of commitments and is intended to speak directly to the familiar charge that commitments are an alien intrusion in and a subversion of the educational process. Only if this issue is at least provisionally settled is it possible to look with some openness at what it might mean to make the kinds of commitments that can, in fact, enrich the educational enterprise. The essays in Part I are arranged in order of increasing specificity: first, the philosophical issue of the relation between objectivity and commitment; next, the question of whether any social institution may properly be said to commit itself; then the kind of commitment that is generic to institutions of liberal learning; and finally, the peculiar commitments that mark a Christian liberal arts college.

Part II deals with commitments and the dimensions of learning. Here the burden of argument is that, taken seriously, a college's commitments enlarge and give completeness to the educational experience, whereas a refusal to take commitments seriously flattens out, formalizes, even trivializes, learning. Consideration is given in separate essays to the dimensions that commitments add to truth, to reality, to cognition, to teaching and learning, and to the quality of the educational experience.

Part III suggests some norms and models of commit-

ment. If institutional commitments are to be made
thoughtfully and with consistency, they must stand in some
comprehensive conceptual framework. Biblical realism
and the concept of Christian ethical community provide
two distinct, though by no means unrelated, ways of approaching and ordering a college's commitments so that
they have organic wholeness. And finally, specific proposals are made for ideological pluralism, on the one hand,
and ideological singularity, on the other.

The reader will quickly discover that there is some
repetition of themes in these essays, though the editors
believe that it is a useful repetition. No two authors coincide in their descriptions or analyses of the issues, and it is
helpful to have several persons who are circling the same
phenomenon say what they see. At the same time, there
is by no means unanimity in the views of our several
essayists. Though all do agree on the importance of clear,
relevant, and wise commitments, not all are agreed on what
commitments are wisest; nor are they of one mind on what
it ought to mean to take seriously even those commitments
on which they do agree. Perhaps this demonstrates that
the critics are simply mistaken when they charge that
commitments generate stylistic conformity and intellectual
stultification.

Limitations of space required that all of the essays that
have appeared in print elsewhere be abridged for use in this
volume. Although this caused the editors the usual amount
of anguish because of the necessity to omit much that is
of genuine interest and merit, they believe that the arguments of individual authors have been preserved with integrity. Only material that was clearly dated, or purely
illustrative, or not essential to the full statement of the
argument, was eliminated. Readers are invited to consult

the essays in their original forms, as noted in the acknowl-edgments, for an even fuller statement and for biblio-graphical citations that could not be reproduced here.

The editors wish to express appreciation for assistance in the preparation of the manuscript to Marti Patchell and Laurie Fifield, successively secretaries to Mr. Jellema; to Mabel Phares, secretary to Mr. Averill; and to Carol White Averill, upon whom fell the major burden of preparing the final typescript for the publisher.

If these essays serve to provoke and clarify significant educational issues, and if they make any contribution at all to the critical examination and deepening of institutional commitments, they will have fulfilled the purpose of the editors in drawing them together.

Commitment Reconstructed

Archibald MacLeish warned, not long ago, of the "diminishment of man" that is at work in our culture. No institution of higher learning—especially no liberal arts college—can be indifferent or give assent to this depletion of the human which has commonly marked our emergence into urban-technical society. To do so would be to destroy the college's reason for existence. Such schools have traditionally justified themselves by the claim to be humane centers of learning, committed to the goal of human wholeness. What is needed now in the colleges is a new thoughtfulness and a new clarity about the humane aims of education. Only in a renewed and fully conscious commitment to human wholeness can they find "values beyond technology," to use the words of the essay that follows. A college will effectively serve the recovery of the humane in the larger society only by determining, itself, to become a more human society. Thoughtfulness and clarity alike are the qualities of this essay by Kenneth Keniston on reconstructing our commitments. And although Keniston was not writing primarily about the colleges, his delineation of human wholeness is a reliable guide by which American colleges can transform old pieties into fresh incarnations.

Kenneth Keniston is Associate Professor of Psychology in the Department of Psychiatry, Yale University.

Kenneth Keniston
Commitment Reconstructed

H istory sometimes presents societies with genuine turning points, eras when men are collectively confronted with a real alternative, ages when crucial decisions can be made which will affect the future for many generations to come. At some such forks in the historical road, men take what later generations will judge the wrong turn, or merely stand bewildered before the alternatives which confront them. In other eras, men choose wisely and well, acting from a courage that permits them to move forward, an understanding that enables them to refuse stagnation. Usually, such eras of potential choice are evident in a widespread sense of historical loss, a feeling that existing values and institutions no longer seem adequate, a realization that men live uneasily with values that now seem empty. In such eras, disquiet and uneasiness pervade men's lives, a nameless dissatisfaction and an even more inarticulate sense of hope for change.

We are approaching, I believe, a new turning point in American society. Despite our growing affluence, despite the triumphant march of technology, despite the inundation of our society with innovations, something is clearly

Abridged from *The Uncommitted*, © 1962, 1965, by Kenneth Keniston, by permission of Harcourt Brace Jovanovich, Inc.

wrong. All the signs are present: our mid-century malaise, increasingly shrill cries to "rededicate" ourselves to outworn ideologies which can no longer inspire our commitment, a loss in the sense of social power, and all of the attitudes, feelings, and outlooks I have here called the "new alienation." The vision of an affluent society no longer excites us, and so, too, we are losing our implicit faith in the ancillary beliefs of technology. In nations where affluence is still a distant dream, the situation is different: in Peru and Nigeria, in Thailand and Samoa, the struggle to attain some small freedom from suffocating poverty is still a compelling struggle. Nor is the achievement of affluence complete even in America: the spate of recent books on the "forgotten fifth" of the nation, on our "invisible poor," eloquently documents the distance we must still travel. Yet these same books, with their appeal for affluence for *all*, indirectly attest to the triumph of technology. Who, a century ago, would have complained that *only* 80 percent of the people were prosperous? And who would have dared insist that *all* might be well fed, well housed, well educated, and well leisured?

Thus, paradoxically, at the very moment when affluence is within our reach, we have grown discontented, confused, and aimless. The "new alienation" is a symptom and an expression of our current crisis. The individual and social roots of our modern alienation, I have tried to suggest, are complex and interrelated; yet if there is any one crucial factor at the center of this alienation, it is the growing bankruptcy of technological values and visions. If we are to move toward a society that is less alienating, that releases rather than imprisons the energies of the dissident, that is truly worthy of dedication, devotion, idealism, and commitment, we must transcend our outworn visions of technological abundance, seeking new values beyond technology.

Paradoxically, then, we live in a society in which un-precedented rates of technological change are accompanied by a fundamental unwillingness to look beyond the technological process which spurs this change. Even those who are most concerned over the future course of our society continue to conceive that course in primarily technological terms, emphasizing quantity, comparisons, economic output, and dollars and cents. And the imagination and commitment needed to define a future qualitatively different from the technological present are deflected—even for those most concerned with our social future—by a series of specific fallacies about the social process.

The Fallacy of the Psychosocial Vise. A characteristic conviction of many modern men and women is the sense of being trapped in a social, cultural, and historical process they have no power to control. This sense of being inescapably locked in a psychosocial vise is often most paralyzing to precisely those men and women who have the greatest understanding of the complexity of their society, and who therefore might be best able to plan intelligently for its future. And although the sense of being trapped in history is widespread, it often appears to receive particularly cogent justification by social scientists. Recent years have seen a growing understanding of the connections between individual character, social process, cultural configuration, and historical change. Just as psychoanalysis has shown that even the most aberrant behavior "makes psychological sense" and serves definable psychic ends, so sociologists argue that social patterns that seem senseless also make a kind of sociological sense, serving "latent functions" corresponding to the unstated needs of individuals. We now know that the link between how men are raised as children and how they lead their lives as adults is a close one, that small changes in one sector of society can have enormous repercussions in other areas, and that apparently small historical transformations may spread and generalize to transform an entire community.

In practice, the fallacy of the psychosocial vise can lead to either despair or complacency.

To be sure, all social planning must be undertaken with the greatest possible understanding of its likely consequences. And we are probably in a better position than any previous generation to assess and gauge what these consequences will be. But the obvious fact that changes in one area of society have repercussions in others need not prevent social action. On the contrary, an understanding of the complexity of society can be an aid to social planning, helping us identify those points and moments of maximum leverage where the small actions can have large consequences. There is often a kind of social "multiplier effect"; there are virtuous as well as vicious circles. Far from discouraging social planning and action, an understanding of psychosocial process can help us guide and direct it more intelligently.

The Fallacy of Romantic Regression. One of the most common reactions against technological society is to deplore it by invoking images of a romanticized past as a guidepost for regressive social change. In future years, as at present, Americans will be increasingly called upon to accept or reject the ideology of romantic regression. This ideology starts from the valid observation that our post-industrial society has lost intact community, socially given identity, stable and accepted morality, certainty, and a clear collective sense of direction. From this valid observation, the regressive position attempts to reestablish a simple "organic" community, longs for Jeffersonian agrarianism, seeks a "new conservatism" which will "preserve" the values of the nineteenth century, turns to Fascism with its appeal to blood feeling and the "corporate state," or is tempted by the syndicalist vision of reattaining "genuine" self-governing communities of workers. All of these outlooks see the solution to the problems of postindustrial society as some form of restoration, re-creation, or reconstruction of the simpler, more intact world that technology has destroyed.

Given a romantic idealization of the past, programs for social action invariably have regressive aims: to *reduce* the complexity of the world, be it material or moral; to *limit* the choices and opportunities which now bewilder men; to *inhibit* freedoms to which men owe their modern anxieties; to *narrow* the alternatives which give rise to current indecision; to *constrain* those who complicate moral, social, political, and international life; to *simplify* moral dilemmas into clear-cut decisions between good and evil. In short, the romantic seeks to solve the problems of the modern world by regressing to his image of an earlier world where these problems did not exist—be it the New England village, the grit-and-gumption ethic of the nineteenth-century entrepreneur, or even the Polynesian island.

However instructive the comparison of our own society with "intact" communities may be, today's problems cannot be solved by regressing to that kind of society. The new problems, the new alienations of technological society, require not regression to a romanticized past but new definitions of purpose, new forms of social organization, new goals for personal development. We must not return to the past but transcend the present.

The Fallacy of Unfinished Business. Perhaps the most

potent deterrent of all to any fresh thinking about the purposes of our lives and our society is the fallacy of unfinished
business—exclusive concentration on the remaining problems of productivity, poverty, education, and inequality as
defined by technological values.

I do not mean to deprecate this position. It is not wrong
but inadequate; the evils pointed to are real and urgent.

But the fallacy of unfinished business overlooks the
crucial questions for most Americans today: What lies
beyond the triumph of technology? After racial equality
has been achieved, what then? Abundance for all for
what? Full employment for today's empty jobs? More
education that instills an ever more cognitive outlook?

It is all too easy to imagine a society in which the triumph
of technology is complete. It would be an overwhelmingly
rich society, dominated by a rampant technology and all
of its corollaries—science, research and development, ad-
vertising, "conformity," secret invidiousness, overwhelming
nostalgia for childhood, the dictatorship of the ego, a continuing deflection of the utopian spirit. It would be a
prosperous, ugly, sprawling society which men had learned
not to see. It would have many entertainers but few artists,
many superhighways but few open spaces to go to on them.
It would be a science-fiction dream of automation, pre-
processing, and home-care conveniences. Skyscrapers
would rise even taller and more sheer, and "developments"
would burgeon outside the blighted urban cores.

Yet the central problems of today would merely be
magnified. The pace of social change would increase, and
without an overall sense of direction, Americans would
huddle ever more defensively in the present. For some,
the romanticized stability of the past would grow more
and more attractive, and this attraction would express itself

more and more forcibly in political and social reaction.
Life, already divided today, would be further divided tomorrow; and the vast majority of Americans, who could
create no community within their hearts, would be altogether without a home. As the pressures toward cognition
grew, private escapes into irrationality, cults, and fads
would flourish. The atmosphere would become ever more
hostile to speculation, to idealism, and to utopianism; the
cult of efficiency, spread into human relations and industrial management, would relegate idealism and the
noble dreams of youth to the hours after work or to "enter-
tainment." In such a society the most talented would be
alienated, yet they would be unable to find a positive voice;
and their alienations would be, as now, self-destructive,
carping, and self-defeating. To complete our incomplete
revolutions, to finish our unfinished business, is therefore
not enough, nor can it be accomplished by technological
means alone. For their solution, the vestigial tasks of technology require values beyond technology.

Toward a More Human Society

If we are to seek values beyond technology, purposes beyond affluence, visions of the good life beyond material
prosperity, where are these values, purposes, and visions
to be found? Must we, as many secretly fear, await the
coming of some new prophet who will create, out of
nothing, a new utopian vision for Americans? Are we
condemned to a continuation of technological society until
some messiah arrives to save us?

I believe the answer is closer to home. When, a century
ago, Americans began to take seriously the goals of prosperity and freedom from want, these values were not

created out of nothing: they had long been part of the Western tradition. What changed was that a dream of the good life previously considered beyond the reach of the ordinary man passed into his hands and was accepted as a concrete goal that could be achieved by ordinary men and women. The turning point at which we stand today requires a similar translation of already existing dreams of human fulfillment and social diversity into the concrete goals of individuals and of our society. The values we need are deeply rooted in our own tradition: we must merely begin to take them seriously.

The ideal of full human wholeness is as old as Periclean Athens. But in the course of Western history, this goal could be taken seriously by few men and women: as in Athens, only a small number of the leisured and wealthy, supported by the vast majority of men and women who were far too preoccupied by their incessant struggle against poverty, oppression, and sickness to have time for such lofty ideals. And even today, for most citizens of most nations of the world, the vision of a more harmonious integration of self, a more complete development of talent and ability, must await the attainment of more urgent goals of attaining freedom from want and oppression. Only those who have been able to conquer poverty and tyranny have energy to cultivate their full humanity.

To be sure, by the quantitative and reductionistic standards of our technological era, goals like "human wholeness," "personal integration," "the full development of human potentials," are inevitably vague and imprecise.

But though no single definition of human fulfillment is possible, some of its results can be defined. A whole man or woman has the capacity for zest, exuberance, and passion, though this capacity may often be in abeyance. An integrated man does not cease to experience tension, anxiety, and psychic pain, but he is rarely overwhelmed by it. Though all men must at times "close" themselves to that which would be subversive of their commitments, a whole man nonetheless retains the *capacity* for openness, sensitivity, and responsiveness to the world around him: he can always be surprised because he remains open to that which is alien to him.

Above all, human wholeness means a capacity for commitment, dedication, passionate concern, and care—a capacity for wholeheartedness and single-mindedness, for abandon without fear of self-annihilation and loss of identity. In psychological terms, this means that a whole man retains contact with his deepest passions at the same time that he remains responsive to his ethical sense. No one psychic potential destroys or subverts the others: his cognitive abilities remain in the service of his commitments, not vice versa; his ethical sense guides rather than tyrannizes over his basic passions; his deepest drives are the sources of his strength but not the dictators of his action. We recognize whole men and women because their wholeness is manifest in their lives: what they do is "of a piece."

The Reconstruction of Commitment

History is always made by men, even in an era like ours when men feel they are but the pawns of history. The inability to envision a future different from the present is not a historical imposition but a failure of imagination. It is individuals, not historic trends, that are possessed by a self-confirming sense of social powerlessness. The decision to continue along our present course rather than to take a new turning is still a decision made by men. One way men sometimes have of shaping the future is to be passive and acquiescent before it. Our collective and individual future, then, will inevitably be shaped by us, whether we choose inaction and passivity, regression and romanticism, or action, imagination, and resolve. Men cannot escape their historical role by merely denying its existence. The question is therefore not *whether* Americans will shape their future but *how* they will shape it.

What is lacking today in America is certainly not the know-how, the imagination, or the intelligence to shape a future better than our present. Nor do we lack the values that might guide the transformation of our society to a more fully human and diverse one. Rather, we lack the conviction that these values might be implemented by ordinary men and women acting in concert for their common good. The utopian impulse, I have argued, runs deep in all human life, and especially deep in American life. What is needed is to free that impulse once again, to redirect it toward the creation of a better society. We too often attempt to patch up our threadbare values and outworn purposes; we too rarely dare imagine a society radically different from our own.

Proposals for specific reforms are bound to be inadequate by themselves. However desirable, any specific reform will remain an empty intellectual exercise in the absence of a new collective myth, ideology, or utopian vision. Politically, no potent or lasting change will be possible except as men can be roused from their current alienations by the vision of an attainable society more inviting than that in which they now listlessly live. Behind the need for any specific reform lies the greater need to create an intellectual, ideological, and cultural atmosphere in which it is possible for men to attempt affirmation without undue fear that their utopian visions will collapse through neglect, ridicule, or their own inherent errors. Such an ethos can only be built slowly and piecemeal, yet it is clear what some of its prerequisites must be.

For one, we need a more generous tolerance for synthetic and constructive ideas. Instead of concentrating on the possible bad motives from which they might arise (the genetic fallacy) or on the possible bad consequences which might follow from their misinterpretation (the progenitive fallacy), we must learn to assess them in terms of their present relevance and appropriateness. To accomplish this task will be a double work. Destructively, it will require subverting the methodologies of reduction that now dominate our intellectual life. Constructively, it will require replacing these with more just measures of relevance, subtlety, and wisdom, learning to cherish and value the enriching complexity of motives, passions, ethical interests, and facts which will necessarily underlie and support any future vision of the good life.

Secondly, we must reappraise our current concepts and interpretations of man and society. It is characteristic of the intellectual stagnation of our era, an era so obviously different from former times, that we continue to operate with language more appropriate to past generations than to our own. Many of our critiques and interpretations of technological society, including most discussions of alienation, apply more accurately to the America of the 1880's than to the America of the 1960's. We require a radical reanalysis of the human and social present—a reevaluation which, starting from uncritical openness to the experience, joys, and dissatisfactions of men today, can gradually develop concepts and theories that can more completely comprehend today's world. American society does not lack men and women with the fine discrimination, keen intelligence, and imagination to understand the modern world, but we have yet to focus these talents on our contemporary problems.

But above and beyond a more generous atmosphere and a more adequate understanding of our time, ordinary human courage is needed. To criticize one's society openly requires a strong heart, especially when criticism is interpreted as pathology: only a man of high mettle will propose a new interpretation of the facts now arranged in entrenched categories. And no matter how eagerly the audience awaits or how well prepared the set, only courage can take a performer to stage. There are many kinds of courages. Needed here is the courage to risk being wrong, to risk doing unintentional harm, and, above all, the courage to overcome one's own humility and sense of finite inadequacy. This is not merely a diffuse "courage to be," without protest, in a world of uncertainty, alienation, and anxiety, but the courage to be *for* something despite the perishability and transience of all human endeavors.

Commitment, I have said, is worthy only as its object is worthy. To try to "reconstruct" commitment to American society as it exists today is less than worthy, for our society is shot through with failings, failures, and flaws. It is, as the alienated truly perceive, "trashy, cheap, and commercial"; it is also, as the alienated seldom see, unjust, distorting of human growth and dignity, destructive of diversity. It has allowed itself to be dominated by the instruments of its own triumph over poverty and want, worshiping the values, virtues, and institutions of technology even when these now dominate those they should serve. Only if we can transform the technological process from a master to a servant, harnessing our scientific inventiveness and industrial productivity to the promotion of human fulfillment, will our society be worthy of commitment. And only the vision of a world beyond technology can now inspire the commitment of whole men and women.

America today possesses a vast reservoir of thwarted and displaced idealism; there are millions of men and women who sense vaguely that something is amiss in their lives, who search for something more, and yet who cannot find it. Their idealism will not be easily redirected to the creation of better lives in a better society; it will require imagination, vigor, conviction, and strong voices willing to call for many years, before we dare raise our aspirations beyond vistas of total technology to visions of fuller humanity. But for the first time in American history, and probably in the history of the world, it is conceivable that a whole nation might come to take seriously these ancient and honored visions.

In defining this new vision of life and society, we must remember the quests of the alienated. Though their goals are often confused and inarticulate, they converge on a passionate yearning for openness and immediacy of experience, on an intense desire to create, on a longing to express their perception of the world, and, above all, on a quest for values and commitments that will give their lives coherence. The alienated of modern American life are often self-defeating; they cannot be taken as exemplars of human integration or fulfillment. But the implicit goals they unsuccessfully seek to attain *are* those of integrated and whole men—openness, creativity, and dedication. Today we need men and women with the wisdom, passion, and courage to transform their private alienations into such public aspirations. We might then begin to move toward a society where such aspirations are more fully realized than in any the world has known.

We can hope for such new commitments in the future

only if men now begin to resolve their alienations by committing themselves—through the analysis, synthesis, and reform of their own lives and worlds—to the preparation of such a new society, a society in which whole men and women can play with zest and spontaneity, can work with skill and dedication, can love with passion and care—a society that enjoys diversity and supports human fulfillment.

Part I
THE NATURE
AND LEGITIMACY
OF COMMITMENTS

CHAPTER 1

Objectivity vs. Commitment

EDITOR'S INTRODUCTION

A professor of history once remarked that he would not trust the reliability of any account of the Reformation written by a Protestant or a Roman Catholic. He was sure that either religious commitment would fatally compromise historical judgment. In his view, only those devoid of any religious commitment whatsoever could be trusted to supply a balanced estimate of the Reformation. Two assumptions stand out in such a view: one is that the religiously uncommitted historian has no biases on religious matters; the second is that commitment is always antithetical to objective scholarship. Huston Smith disagrees persuasively on both points. In scholarship, he contends, objectivity and neutrality, in the sense of presuppositionless and value-free inquiry, are alike impossible. But more than that, he holds that belief supplies that confidence which is "the *sine qua non* of the open mind." If Smith is right—and his essay is here because the editors believe he is—that may explain why much American higher education is so nondescript these days. It has embraced a philosophy of "pluralism," which sounds intellectually virtuous, but which turns out on examination to be only disintegration. Commitment critically held—conviction that is marked as genuine by its fairness to evidence—can become the source of new distinctiveness and vigor in education.

Huston Smith is Professor of Philosophy in the Massachusetts Institute of Technology.

Huston Smith
Objectivity vs. Commitment

THE DICHOTOMY THAT CONCERNS US HERE MIGHT BE EXPRESSED in several other ways: open-mindedness versus conviction, disinterestedness versus concern, impartiality versus partisanship, detachment versus attachment. However formulated, it presents a tension between our need to believe and our concern to keep our beliefs from standing between us and the truth.

The Dangers of Attachment and the Search for Objectivity

The evils that spring from partisanship, commitment, and unshakable conviction are well known. Emotions have

Abridgment of "Objectivity and Commitment," from *The Purposes of Higher Education*, by Huston Smith. Copyright 1955, by Harper & Row, Publishers, Inc. Reprinted by permission of the publishers.

proved themselves to be a perennial source of bias. Attachments to established points of view block the emergence of new insights; attachments to personal interests block the common good. Not only do such biases cause uncongenial evidence to be suppressed; what is worse, they distort the way evidence actually looks.

The natural reaction to these dangers is to reject attachments altogether and to take up the ideal of complete detachment or disinterestedness. Thus there has sprung up in our undergraduate and graduate schools, as well as in our professional societies, a cult of "robust skepticism." Its unwritten charter can be abbreviated as follows: The most important ingredient in the intellectual venture is objectivity, the mind's innocence and transparency before the facts. Since convictions, beliefs, and commitments involve emotional attachments, they necessarily interfere with this transparency. So, on the altar of objectivity, they must be sacrificed.

Let us notice two things about this platform before we examine it systematically: first, the high price which objectivity exacts when thus defined in opposition to belief. Is it possible for a people to live together, let alone live well together, unless their lives are ordered beyond the crude reaches of the law by a substantial set of common values and beliefs? If objectivity does require diluting our personal and collective concerns, the cure for bias may well be worse than the disease. Second, we need to realize that the position of the teacher in society makes it easy for him to decide this question irresponsibly if he is not careful. He does not have to assume responsibility for directing the course of society—for rallying a people to decision, say, in an hour of crisis. He does not even have to assume responsibility for the total life of his students. Moreover, he is working with adolescents and near adolescents to whom the sweetest music is often the sound of falling idols. Administrators, psychiatrists, and spiritual directors never for a moment question the importance of convictions and commitments. That educators sometimes do may indicate greater perspicacity and sophistication; on the other hand it may indicate that they are playing a pet peeve or laboring a private advantage instead of responding to the rounded needs of the individual and society. It is important that we discover which, lest our culture, looking to its schools for wisdom, receive in its place harassment.

With the seriousness of the question before us, let us try to discover what the proponents of objectivity are after. Perhaps what they really want is not as inimical to belief as it at first appears.

Is Complete Objectivity Possible?

If we understand by pure objectivity a state of affairs in which the mind mirrors the facts without disturbing or re-arranging them in any way, it is an ideal which man's mind can never achieve. H. A. Hodges, professor of philosophy in the University of Reading, has summarized several of the most important factors which make it humanly impossible for the mind to reflect the events of nature without some refraction.[1] We can adapt his points as follows:

1. *Interpretation*. All thinking imposes an order of some sort upon sense data which would otherwise be scattered and unrelated. Our sense impressions do not come to us already structured and ordered, with their meaning written clearly across them. They depend on the mind for their interpretation. The mind is always reading meaning into

nature. On the whole this is a good thing, but it hardly makes for objectivity in its absolute sense.

2. *Selection.* It is impossible to look at, to say nothing of study, everything at once. Selection is at work in all observation and inquiry. But to select is to leave out, so full objectivity again falls by the wayside.

3. *Specialization.* When selection becomes systematic, it passes into specialization, a third barrier to objectivity particularly formidable in higher education. Specialization is, of course, valuable and inevitable if knowledge is to advance as it should. But being by definition the attempt to consider only one phase or aspect of a subject to the deliberate exclusion of others, it can hardly be claimed to contribute to objectivity. "Only the whole truth," F. H. Bradley used to say, "is wholly true." Specialization interferes with objectivity.

4. *Climates of Opinion.* Cultures and historical epochs have their limiting horizons no less than do academic disciplines. We see this more clearly in other peoples, but it is foolish to suppose that we alone are free of limiting perspectives which shut out the full truth. They will be all too plain to our grandchildren who will be amazed and amused at our blindness and earn doctoral degrees tracing the social and historical causes which gave rise to them.

5. *Emotion.* The foregoing blocks to objectivity arise from the very nature of mental activity apart from any interference from the emotions. But the mind is not insulated from the latter: it feels the impact of hates, loves, and fears, and responds to them openly or unconsciously. Freud has shown that the unconscious influence of desires upon thought and imagination is far more pervasive than we had supposed. Nor is it only the violent emotions which color our conclusions: Carl Jung and William

Sheldon have explored the way certain types of personality
appear to give rise to recognizable biases which come out in
both thought and action. Marx, in turn, stressed the way
different social classes develop sets of attitudes which determine their outlooks, individuals taking the mold of the
classes to which they belong.

These five sources of distortion are so inherent in the
mind and its operations that the staunchest objectivist will
admit that it is futile to look forward to overcoming them.
Objectivity, in the pure sense of transcending these limitations, would mean nothing less than a God's-eye view of
reality. Being men, our minds will always be limited, and
limitation involves bias of one sort or another.

It is the last-named distortion, emotion, that continues
to worry the objectivist. The others are inevitable; besides
they seem to enter more as limitations than as active dis-
tortions. But the passions are violent. They can blind
and twist the evidence until objectivity is reduced to
shambles. However, they can be controlled, at least partially. Let us then, having granted that pure objectivity is
out of the question, seek nevertheless to be as objective as
possible by keeping our feelings out of our knowing. The
proposal amounts to a plea for neutrality. It is all right
to have perspectives, but not convictions.

Is Neutrality Possible—Or Desirable?

It is impossible to come to grips with the problem of
neutrality unless we distinguish several principal kinds.

1. *Cognitive Neutrality.* This involves suspending judgment concerning the truth or falsity of statements of fact.
Complete cognitive neutrality is impossible. It is flatly
incompatible with life. The quest for ignorance has been

given a good run—historically from the Greek Skeptics down well past Descartes, individually during some phase in the career of nearly every college student. But it never quite comes off. It goes pretty well in the rarified subtleties of epistemology and metaphysics, but when the philosopher sneezes and finds himself again a man, he discovers on the plane of common sense a number of things he cannot doubt without becoming melodramatic and more than a bit silly —that potatoes are more edible than pebbles, for example, or that he is less likely to get hurt if he leaves for lunch by the first-floor door than by his third-floor window. Doubt things like these and the skeptic reads himself out of existence; and even in his doing so, such is the irony of his lot, he becomes traitor, not martyr, to his cause, for as Pascal remarked, even those who are going to hang themselves do so because they believe it is the best way out. The complete skeptic is a philosopher's fiction. It is possible to dive deep into the sea of doubt, but one never quite touches rock bottom.

2. *Value Neutrality in General.* But perhaps it is not cognitive neutrality which the objectivist is proposing. Certainly, he might admit, with regard to matters of *fact* it is possible to discover where truth lies and foolish not to follow its leads with belief. It is in the area of *values* that all the trouble arises.

This is not the place to enter into the intricate problem of whether questions of value are as distinct from questions of fact as this position supposes. Suffice it to say that value judgments are as inescapable as judgments of fact, so that generalized neutrality here is as impossible and indefensible as in regard to knowledge. Life requires direction, and in human beings no longer maneuvered by instinct this direction can be supplied only by a stable (which is not to say unchanging) nucleus of values and beliefs. Convictions of some sort are the only safeguards against mental bewilderment and moral flabbiness. We are never so much at the mercy of external circumstances as when we are in a state of indecision, never so free as when we have made up our minds, assuming we have made them up well.

Indecision is anything but a blanket virtue: it can indicate indifference, timidity, or weakness of will just as much as open-mindedness. If there are things that ought to be believed, this being the whole meaning of truth, there are also sides that ought to be espoused: this is the burden of goodness. To remain neutral in the face of these, or to be overhesitant in deciding where they lie, is not wisdom but its opposite. G. K. Chesterton declared himself unable to understand how anyone could be impartial about right and wrong. Is it possible that as teachers we have used our duty to present all sides of a question as an excuse for avoiding the responsibility of personal involvement? Certainly there are some who make a point of practicing conscientious indecision. Doubtless they act in good faith. But one suspects that concern has withered from their lives and that objectivity has come to mean not fair play but aloofness. Some even display a perverse pride in being above the raging battles.

The effects of such object lessons on students can only be deadly. For, to repeat, life demands direction. Certainly youth should have a hand in determining this direction—the charts should not be unilaterally dictated from above. But what is not legitimate is for education to sidestep the problem of helping students to clarify goals worthy of commitment. If youth finds its schools uninterested in charts and compasses—if, worse, it finds its teachers never approaching such things save in the partisan (sic!) spirit of a demolition squad—there is but one alternative. Youth will listen to voices outside the campus walls, voices that promise to give life meaning by enlisting it in the service of a political ideology.

3. *Specific Value Neutrality: (a) Toward the Academic Virtues.* Instead of prolonging on an abstract level the argument that complete value neutrality is neither possible nor advisable, let us descend to the level of specifics and ask, "What values would the objectivists have education be neutral toward?" Should it, for example, be neutral to the so-called academic virtues, those qualities of mind and character which mark the serious student and the competent teacher or scholar? One thinks of clarity, openness to evidence, patience, perseverance, an eye for detail, and honesty, to mention a few. Simply to raise this question is to answer it. Certainly no one is suggesting that we turn indifferent to these values. To believe in education is to believe in these things with it.

4. *Specific Value Neutrality: (b) Toward the Social Order.* Agreement in this second area is not so forthcoming. There are many who would argue, for example, that education has no direct concern with political values. Colleges and universities should be in the world but not of it. They should be communities apart, pervaded by an atmosphere of detachment, deliberately removed from the political fray. Of course they play their part in society, but this part is *sui generis.* Its contribution is on a different level, the level of culture, taste, and knowledge, particularly knowledge for its own sake.

This attitude is not without its element of truth. Certainly the atmosphere of a college should be markedly different from that of a city hall, and the purposes of a university clearly distinguishable from those of a political party. Nevertheless, those who argue that education should remain aloof from questions of social policy must be prepared to face two consequences. First, they must stand ready to see education isolated from the mainstream of practical life, and in consequence partially trivialized.

The second danger is that complete social neutrality may contribute to a condition in which education (as we know it) is impossible. We have grim record of this in the experience of European universities preceding and during World War II. Nowhere was the ideal of neutrality more completely enthroned. Majestically these universities moved along their erudite planes, exercising little effect on society at large—they were above such involvement. Small wonder they proved to be completely spineless in the face of Nazi ideology, even when this challenged the very foundations—freedom, objectivity, and respect for truth—on which their existence was predicated. Not only were the German universities a pushover for Hitler; almost without exception those in the occupied countries failed to tie in effectively with resistance movements. The denouement, as we all know, was one of the grimmest in education's entire history: learning cast into chains, scholars enslaved and persecuted, education as we know it replaced with barefaced indoctrination. Do we need a clearer—or closer—object lesson to make us see that education presupposes certain social values? To say that we believe in education without saying also that we believe in these values is to speak words without sense. Can we consistently champion education as we believe in it without championing also the only kind of society which makes possible free thinking and honest teaching, a society in which respect for persons, fair play, and openness to criticism and discussion are deeply ingrained? We can no longer pretend that education is outside politics, for a kind of politics has arisen which is antithetical to all that makes true education possible. True education must perforce be opposed to this kind of politics and do everything in its power to counter it. As teachers we have accepted freedom as a convenience for ourselves and in our work. The time has come when we must make it a part of our faith and champion it as a necessary part of any worthy social order. Any shibboleth about impartiality and nonattachment which beclouds this issue is unworthy of our hour.

5. *Specific Value Neutrality: (c) In Science and Research*. But perhaps we have again done the objectivists an injustice. When they advocate neutrality perhaps they are not thinking of life as whole; their wish may be simply to produce men who, in the words of S. Alexander, "have learned to keep their dislikes out of their science." This is certainly a more reasonable proposal. Indeed, it has great merit. We have all known enough thinkers who load their findings to fit their theories to be rightly suspicious of the type. Yet even here three qualifications concerning neutrality in scholarship and research must be entered: (1) To check our value judgments at the doors of our library or laboratory is easier in some disciplines than in others. Roughly the disciplines arrange themselves in a continuum in this respect, from the physical sciences, through the biological and social sciences, to the humanities. Even in the latter categories one sometimes finds historians who claim to do nothing but "tell what happened" or ethicists who profess to do no more than analyze the value statements of others. But on the whole the less conclusions can be set down in terms of mechanical pointer readings, the more assumptions and interpretations are recognized to enter into these conclusions. (2) Even in the natural sciences,

value judgments cannot be eliminated entirely. They underlie the researcher's confidence in the scientific method, his choice of problem, and the point of view from which it is regarded. (3) We must not let our attention to the way value judgments and convictions can block new truths obscure the less-noticed fact that they can also help bring new truths to light. For do men ever discover an intricately linked series of facts unless these are ordered by a hypothesis they suspect is true? Indeed, if the hypothesis is a subtle one to establish, must not its advocates have a strong conviction of its truth to keep them traveling the long track of verification? If the hypothesis is highly original, its advocates may even have to work for long stretches in the face of conventional interpretations which may look like negative evidence. We can only wonder how many corpses of promising hypotheses lie strewn beside the gates of education, prematurely dead because someone lacked faith in their future sufficient to continue to nourish them. The warning is against cutting off possibly creative convictions with oversimple, cut-and-dried slogans about keeping our values out of our science. We need to realize the extent to which the canons of what we call knowledge are saturated with interpretation; this will help us to encourage rather than excommunicate those creative thinkers who are on the verge of something—exploring hypotheses which, if substantiated, will crack our present modes of thought and carry us into the waiting wonderland of the unforeseen.

The Constructive Meaning of Objectivity

We have been asking what objectivity, defined in opposition to beliefs and convictions, can reasonably mean, and we have not found an answer.

Are we to conclude then that this ideal to which our educational institutions are so deeply attached has no valid meaning? We cannot believe that this is so. It is more likely that in our discussion thus far we have misconceived what objectivity really means. We have been working from the assumption that objectivity implies neutrality and so is antithetical to belief and conviction. Perhaps this is not true. We have seen that objectivity must always operate in a context of some beliefs and convictions. It may be that the two are not intrinsically opposed at all, in other words, that the depth of conviction in a man can lead us to predict nothing about the openness of his mind. If so, it will be feasible to try to produce men who believe well and are objective at the same time.

Let us ask again what the objectivist really wants, now that some of the prevalent interpretations of his position turn out to be inadequate. He is not basically after negative things like absence of beliefs or commitments. What he wants is a positive virtue which can be described quite simply as fairness to evidence. This involves open-mindedness—the willingness, even eagerness, to entertain seriously every item of relevant evidence that has a bearing on the problem at hand. It involves maximum responsiveness to the facts, seeing each, as far as possible, with discrimination and without distortion to the end that it may be assigned its appropriate and becoming weight.

Defined thus in positive instead of negative terms, objectivity is a wonderful virtue. Every educator will subscribe to it with all his heart. Keeping hold of this constructive meaning, let us now go on to ask how it is related to the beliefs and convictions which life must also harbor. If the two sets of attitudes turn out to be compatible, we shall have risen above the frustrating dichotomy of attachment versus detachment to a synthesis widely acceptable among the diverse wings of contemporary education.

The Relation of Objectivity to Belief

We must begin by acknowledging that objectivity and belief *can* be in sharp tension, even direct conflict. Under certain psychological conditions—they may even be the most usual ones—belief releases three powerful springs which can snap closed the most open mind. One of these is fear. To the extent that my belief is important to me, I am likely to shrink from evidence which might upset it. The second is complacency. We are all acquainted with what John Stuart Mill referred to as "the deep slumber of a settled opinion." To the extent that I really believe something is true, I shall be satisfied with it and write off the need for looking into further evidence. The third spring which pulls shut the open mind is pride. Men seldom have the lowliness to receive from all quarters. Instead they develop possessive interests in their theories and fence out all possible poachers. Indeed, they often come to look upon their theories as not only their own but as part of themselves, feeling personal affront if they are challenged or punctured.

Obviously the tensions that can arise between belief on the one hand and objectivity on the other are very real. But now we come to an interesting and less recognized point. Far from being incompatible with conviction, open-mindedness and objectivity actually are the chief marks of its genuineness. Imagine an article of faith which I regard as crucial to my well-being. To the extent that I am really convinced that it is true, I will have no fear that further evidence will undermine it; I will be relaxed and eager to examine additional information and will feel no compulsive need to interpret this information in line with my established preconceptions. For, to repeat, to the extent that I really believe it is true I will also believe that additional evidence will confirm and strengthen my conviction rather than destroy it. Conversely, the least fear and shrinking from evidence will indicate that consciously or subconsciously I already doubt that my belief can square with truth. Dogmatism is always a substitute for self-confidence.

The Open Self as Matrix for Responsible Commitment

There is, however, another level to this matter. It is perfectly true that to the extent that I have faith in a specific proposition I will be open-minded about it. But there is another kind of faith, faith of a different order, which belongs not so much to the mind as to the total man. This faith does not reside in the cerebral cortex but in the total character structure of the personality. It does not attach iself to specific doctrines; instead it is a generalized orientation toward the world as a whole and all life. It is the basic quality of what we may call the open self. In science it takes the form of confidence that any particular hypothesis which falls will be superseded by a more adequate and inclusive one. In religion it takes the form of confidence that if any specific article of faith must go, this is to make room for vaster and more creative insights. In both cases basic faith makes it possible for the individual to face without fear the prospect of permanent revolution on the level of his specific ideas.

How this basic faith comes is largely a mystery, though

early environment seems to have a good deal to do with it. Two things, however, are clear. When it does come it is an unmixed blessing. And second, it provides that matrix of ultimate confidence toward life which can accommodate the maximum open-mindedness. For it makes it unnecessary for the individual to dig in, draw the battlelines, and stand or fall by any specific doctrine. Doctrinal defensiveness and overprotection are unneeded, for security is no longer structured on this brittle level. One has found the secret of inner confidence, and with it the greatest leverage for the open mind which life can afford.

Fallibilism as the Complement to Confidence in the Open Self

We have now been brought to a paradox: the more faith a person has, the more open-minded he will be. In one sense this is perfectly true. Any increase in confidence, whether it be confidence in a specific proposition or confidence toward life in general, automatically reduces one of the three great barriers to open-mindedness—fear. Unfortunately it does little or nothing to remove the other two, complacency and intellectual pride. Because these content us with our existing beliefs, they slack our search for new evidence, and should this evidence emerge on its own, they usually blunt its force by causing us to interpret it in ways favorable to beliefs already enthroned.

Pride and complacency are overcome by something that looks at first as if it were the exact opposite of confidence but turns out simply to lie at right angles to it in a different dimension, as it were. We can call this something "fallibilism." Fallibilism is the vivid awareness of the mind's limitations, the high sense of the finitude of every human perspective. It need not be depressing. To realize how little the mind knows compared with what it might know is more likely to be exhilarating than the opposite, for our final concern is with reality as a whole, not just that fragment which our mind has already seized. The truly depressing view is the one which sees the world as consisting of nothing but what our brains have already digested and partially deflavored—mental cud, Koheleth's image of a world in which there is "nothing new under the sun." Fallibilism is a creed for adventurers. Agreeing with Sir Thomas Browne that "the hypothesis of yesterday is the theory of today, the accepted doctrine of tomorrow, and the fallacy of the future," it feeds on a lively awareness of the transitional character of every idea and perspective. It knows that the mind's immediate content, like the manna in the hands of the Israelites, cannot be kept: it is the bread which man must eat at the present stage of his journey through the wilderness of ignorance. He must go on in faith that for each stage of his growth an appropriate "bread of the day" and of the coming day awaits him. "Orthodoxy is the wealth of today," it has been said, "but it is heresy which holds tomorrow in its hand." Those who have seen this can go forward regarding their current perspectives as a little more earthly than eternal verities, seeing them instead as hypotheses by which it is good to live but which we will want to abandon or modify as future evidence should indicate. Those who can gladly and wholeheartedly embrace fallibilism in this sense have the safest protection known against what Radhakrishnan calls "the bondage of a final creed." They have an objectivity which springs from the mind's knowledge of its own subjectivity. They have an insurance against the hazards of complacency and intellectual pride.

It is in connection with fallibilism that one of the most ticklish questions concerning the relation between open-mindedness and conviction arises. We may put it this way: Does not fallibilism necessarily curb the depth of conviction? Is it not a contradiction to give full assent to something which one suspects contains an element of error? If these questions must be answered in the affirmative, we have been romantic in our praise of fallibilism, for it is unlikely that any outlook which shortens the reach of man's possible conviction is sound.

A simple distinction will help as much as anything to answer the questions before us. It is the difference between advancing in the direction you have been going, and backtracking. In both cases there is movement, but the kinds are antithetical. With ideas there is a similar difference: they can be reversed or advanced. Fallibilism expects that every idea will move, but this does not mean that all will reverse their present direction. I may believe with all my heart that love is better than hate, or truth than falsehood. The finitude of all human perspectives does not require me to expect that time will reverse these beliefs. All it says is that my present understanding of love and truth is imperfect and new insight will add to it. Whether additional insights will reverse my present perspectives or enlarge, clarify, and refine them, is a question on which fallibilism says nothing one way or the other. The answer to that question depends entirely on how true my preliminary beliefs have been set.

In short, ideas are subject to two kinds of failings: they can be wrong or they can be incomplete. Fallibilism involves a lively sense that all our ideas are incomplete, but it does not require the positive feeling that all are wrong. On the latter point it expects us to be open-minded in the sense of being ready to consider any evidence which suggests that our beliefs are mistaken, but until such evidence comes along we are entitled to be as confident as we please of the direction in which they point.

I heard recently of a student in Kansas who went to his adviser. He was troubled by entering a course on education and having the teacher write in large letters across the blackboard, "NO ABSOLUTES." The teacher continued by taking the first hour to explain that this was to be the underlying premise of the course. I do not know what the explanation included, but what it should have included (and from the student's reported reaction I suspect did not) was a clear distinction among four things:

1. Absolutes held dogmatically: Psychological factors make us refuse to consider negative evidence and the possibility that we may be mistaken (always bad).

2. Absolutes accepted as finalities: Our absolute takes care of the problem completely, so there is no need to refine, enlarge, or deepen our current understanding (always bad).

3. Absolutes extended beyond their appropriate contexts (always bad).

4. Absolutes which, without being held either dogmatically or as finalities, and without neglect of their appropriate contexts, elicit our complete conviction because all the evidence we have been able to discover supports them. We will be happy to consider any contrary evidence which anyone can offer, and we certainly do not feel that we understand the full implications of our present view. But the drift of evidence, as we have been given to see this evidence, has been such that we expect further material to confirm and clarify rather than reverse what we already hold to be true. (Can be good, depending on the beliefs in question. Belief in the value of truth, goodwill, open-

mindedness, freedom, democracy, and individual worth might be examples of absolutes valid in this sense.)

With this clarification of the meaning of fallibilism, we can return to the questions which introduced it. Does not fallibilism necessarily curb the depth of conviction? The answer is, No. Is it not a contradiction to give full assent to something which one suspects contains an element of error? The answer is, Yes, but fallibilism does not require that we suspect all our beliefs of error, only of incompleteness.

We are now in a position to suggest the way in which the various psychological components we have been discussing—fear, complacency, pride, confidence, fallibilism, warranted belief, and dogmatism—can be related to produce a reliable context for responsible belief.

The most important piece in the puzzle is basic confidence, a pervading security toward life and the world in general. Such confidence is the *sine qua non* of the open mind. Without it our minds will be rigid, intolerant, savagely repellent to new knowledge, and every mince in the direction of objectivity will be a concession. With it, we can ride each wave of incoming knowledge, in a spirit rightly identified with adventure, pushing out with new tolerance and fresh curiosity on wider seas of comprehension.

After confidence comes fallibilism. Confidence makes fallibilism possible. It gives an amplitude and flexibility to the mind which heightens its tolerance toward tentativity, doubt, and uncertainty. Insecure persons must reinforce their precarious stability with certainties, absolutes, and dogmas of one sort or another; individuals who are basically secure in themselves have no such need. Confidence and fallibilism are the companion prerequisites to the open mind. Together they stave off its principal threats. Confidence counters fear; fallibilism counters complacency and pride.

The Status of Convictions in the Open Self

Confidence and fallibilism, we have seen, are not primarily ideas held in the head; they are traits of the individual's total psychological makeup. They are basic components of the personality in terms of which the individual approaches any specific hypothesis or proposal. But minds do not consist only of tendencies, attitudes, sets, and orientations. They have content as well—specific ideas which are entertained, concrete principles which are believed. What do the ideals of objectivity and open-mindedness propose regarding these?

Not, obviously, that the mind should have no contents. The open mind is not unstocked; it is accessible. Any evidence relevant to the question at hand can find in it a ready audience. But this does not mean that every item of evidence which gains entrance must be given equal weight with every other item. If open-mindedness has nothing to do with empty-mindedness, neither is it wedded to gullibility. Its capacity is to listen, not to swallow. There may well be two sides to every question, but to believe not only that both sides are entitled to a hearing but that they must always be given equal credence is so out of keeping with good sense that it could be held only by an obstinacy the reverse of open-mindedness. Finally, objectivity and open-mindedness do not require that convictions be less than complete in their power to rally the full energies of those who hold them. They do not advise us that it is all right to believe something, but not to be convinced of it.

What objectivity and open-mindedness do require of beliefs is (1) that they be warranted and (2) that they not be held dogmatically.

To say that a belief should be warranted does not mean it must be demonstrable. Some beliefs should be—propositions in geometry, for example, are not worthy of belief unless they can be established by a series of proofs. Wherever demonstration is possible, belief should accord with it. But proof is a scant garment; at best it covers but a fraction of our intellectual nakedness. After logic and the scientific method have done their best we are still faced with the necessity of deciding most of the issues of life in the light of convictions which exceed strict demonstration. Sometimes demonstration carries part of the weight of our convictions but works in terms of premises and assumptions which elude definite proof. Sometimes observations point our beliefs in a given direction but do not constitute a sufficient sample for a high degree of probability. Sometimes evidence seems to be so completely lacking or evenly balanced on two sides of a proposition that we cannot appeal to it at all in support of our stand.

Accordingly, our beliefs will arrange themselves in a continuum, from those which for all practical purposes can be conclusively demonstrated to those which can claim scarcely any balance of evidence in their favor. We must not conclude from this that only those beliefs which are backed by firm evidence are justified. The problem of "warranted belief" is a complicated one. Whether a given belief is warranted cannot be measured simply in terms of the gross quantity of evidence it commands. At least three other factors must be taken into consideration:

1. What portion of the total evidence available on the issue does the part which supports our belief represent?

This is usually more important than the quantity of supporting evidence considered by itself. A simple hunch, slender evidence though it is, can mean more to one belief than a thousand experimental confirmations to another, provided the first belief admits of no further evidence and the second could be tested by more careful sampling than the thousand instances provide. Where virtual certainty is possible (as in the formal sciences) we expect warranted beliefs to command it; where high probability is the order, as in natural science, such probability is enough; where basic intuitions and appraisals count for so much, as in metaphysics and religion, these will often have to do.

2. How urgent is it that we take some stand on the issue at hand? Is suspended judgment possible, or do we have to make up our minds one way or the other? If we were asked out of a clear blue sky whether it rained yesterday in Madrid, no answer we could give would be warranted. Since there is no reason why we have to commit ourselves on such a question, the only sensible thing to do is to withhold judgment until evidence is supplied. When, on the other hand, we turn to what William James called "forced options," the case is changed. Where we have to decide one way or the other, we are prepared to respect beliefs even when supported by the most meager evidence. In cases where you have to add up your findings and act on that summary, it is no use remarking that such a summary is provisional and incomplete. Of course it is, but equally you must act with such knowledge as you have.

3. If the belief turns out to be wrong, how serious will the consequences be? This question, too, will affect the amount of evidence needed to justify a belief. A housewife in setting a table is justified in believing without further test that the substance in her salt shaker is salt, for she has

never made the mistake of filling the shaker with sugar and her children are not given to playing practical jokes. But a pharmaceutical company preparing a potent drug for distribution on the mass market would not be warranted in assuming the nature of one of its intended ingredients without a more careful check.

It is easy to say with a contemporary philosopher and educator, "To believe without proper evidence—that is the greatest sin," but we are merely doctrinaire unless we recognize that a host of life's questions admit of only the most improper evidence judged by any absolute standards. Yet they are among the most important we face, and some answer to them is unavoidable. No interpretation of open-mindedness which stifles conviction on the important questions of life by demanding of them more evidence than they can yield is adequate to the human situation. We need to retain our faith that life can be considerably more reasonable than it is without overlooking the fact that it will probably always remain less logical and "scientific" than we might wish. Intuitive, subjective, and emotional bases of belief will never be eliminated; if we saw the problem in full perspective, we should perhaps be grateful for this instead of annoyed.

We have been discussing the first prerequisite of specific convictions; if they are to be objective and in accord with the open mind, they must be warranted. The second essential is that they not be held dogmatically.

It is right that in speaking of dogmatism we acknowledge that we are all more or less guilty. But this fact does not rob "dogmatic" of objective meaning. While no one can avoid having some prejudices, some people at least see that theirs get exposed and ventilated once in a while, while others keep doors and windows locked as if fresh air carried the plague. With some minds it is astonishingly easy to enter a countersuggestion; with others it is like trying to get a breeze through a billiard ball. Nor, much as we would like to, are we always able to fasten dogmatism to the other side. We meet impressively undogmatic persons whose views differ sharply from our own as well as others whose obstinacy is not obscured by the fact that they happen to agree with us. Several symptoms of dogmatism are by now rather generally recognized, and can be isolated from the conclusions they support. One is open defiance of evidence: Tertullian's "I believe because it is absurd" might be an instance. Another is the attempt to intimidate opposition as, for example, a century ago wickedness of heart was regularly imputed to those who presumed to question the infallibility of the Bible. A third disguise for dogmatism is to insist on the self-evident character of the doctrine in question. Insistence upon self-evidence can easily front as an excuse for not mustering evidence.

Admittedly, "warranted" and "undogmatic" are not easy standards to apply. Yet they have sufficient content to permit us to say that specific convictions are thoroughly compatible with objectivity and open-mindedness if they are warranted and not held dogmatically. The ideal is a person who on the foundations of basic confidence and a keen sense of fallibilism builds a firm structure of specific beliefs. Because they are warranted, he holds them with assurance; but because he is not dogmatic he is happy to reexamine and modify them if necessary in the light of developing evidence.

Two miscellaneous observations bearing upon the relation of detachment and commitment will bring this chapter to a close.

One is that there are two kinds of doubt, constructive

and destructive. Constructive doubt questions existing
opinions when it sees these as obstructing the vision of
more adequate ones. Destructive doubt loves to destroy
for its own sake. Its springs are in nihilism, the intellectual
variant of the suicide impulse. Education should never
succumb to the cliché of glorifying the critical spirit in
general; it should cultivate constructive doubt and reform
the other kind.

The second point has been suggested but should perhaps
be explicitly stated. It is a mistake to draw a sharp line
between science on the one hand and politics, morals, and
religion on the other, contending that doubt and detachment are appropriate in science but of course "in the area
of values" we must have beliefs. Science has convictions
which mean just as much to it as do God, goodwill, and
democracy to the other areas—convictions concerning the
orderliness of nature, for example, or the reliability of the
scientific method. Need we add that conversely religion,
morals, and politics need to hear from time to time "the
still small voice that whispers 'fiddlesticks.'" Neither side
deserves, nor has, a monopoly on either faith or doubt.
There may well be differences in degree between the disciplines on these points; certainly it is more difficult to proceed "purely factually" in those areas where values enter
more directly. But the general principles here outlined
apply to man's knowledge and belief in general with no
difference in principle between science and the value fields.

Summary and Conclusions for Education

The constructive meaning of objectivity does not imply
absence of a point of view nor neutrality toward either
ideas or values. It means respect for evidence which im-

plies open-mindedness, perceptiveness, and the patient attempt to avoid distortion. Tensions can easily develop between objectivity and conviction, but the two can also be compatible. To help make them so is a major responsibility of education, for it is impossible to think either that life can be lived without beliefs or that it can be lived well if beliefs take over without the saving check of objectivity. Beliefs are held objectively if they are warranted by available evidence and are open to revisions in the light of further information. Fear, complacency, and intellectual pride are the chief obstacles to such further revision; they can be countered by basic confidence as a personality trait and a keen awareness of the fallibility of all human perspectives.

Pascal said a man should be able to deny well, to doubt well, and to believe well. Education should help students do all three.

CHAPTER 2

Institutional Commitment: A Social Scientist's View

EDITOR'S INTRODUCTION

When talk turns to colleges and commitments, someone can be counted upon to object that institutions do not function like individuals. A human person may, by means of a centered act, organize his priorities for commitment to some abstract ideal or course of action. But the human analogy, it is argued, is inappropriate where social groups are concerned. An institution is not a centered self, is not capable of the same kind of priority-organizing control, and thus cannot properly be said to "commit" itself. Social scientist Harry Davis disagrees, and he marshals argument from the current literature on social organization in support of his view that, for social institutions as for individuals, commitments are not only possible but inevitable.

Harry R. Davis is Professor of Government in Beloit College.

Harry R. Davis

Institutional Commitment: A Social Scientist's View

The Possibility of Institutional Commitment

It is sometimes argued that "institutional commitment" is an impossibility—that an *institution* as such and because of its very nature cannot "commit" itself. *Individual persons* may, probably ought, perhaps inevitably must (insofar as they behave rationally), commit themselves to basic visions of reality and value systems. But a particular institution is a living entity composed of many diverse individuals, a rich and complex set of relationships responding to a great variety of conflicting pressures and motives. It is not subject to much if any predictability or rational control. Such an entity can hardly make a commitment of its own. Its experience is open-ended: it moves and adapts in dependence on the changing commitments of the individuals who compose it, as well as of those who affect it from outside.

In order to test this thesis, we need a clear understanding of the meaning of "commitment." The relevant definitions from *Webster's Third New International Dictionary* include "the obligation or pledge to carry out some action or policy or to give support to some policy or person" and "the state of being obligated or bound (as by intellectual conviction or emotional ties): a state or declaration of adherence or association (as to a doctrine or ideal)." The question, then, is whether an institution is the kind of being that is capable of declaring its adherence to some doctrine, person, or purpose, and pledging itself to carry out policies in support of its adherence.

The argument that institutional commitment is impossible turns on a particular academic conception of institution—more especially on a sharp if not complete distinction between institution and organization. If by definition only organizations can self-consciously choose their goals and control themselves rationally for the achievement of those goals, and institutions are by contrast defined as unselfconscious and undisciplined entities—then, of course, an easy victory is won.

Certain insights developed in recent years by social scientists appear at first glance to demonstrate support for this definitional distinction. Students of public and business administration have come to recognize that the actual life of a sizable and complex institution embodies far more than the relationships shown on the formal organization chart which may serve as its skeleton. The older "structural" theory of organization involves a well-defined purpose, specialization and functional grouping, coordination, leadership through formal hierarchy and authority, and so on. This understanding has now been supplemented by a more "behavioral" theory of institutional life which emphasizes a variety of more "human" factors such as informal leadership, personal motivations that may conflict with official goals, decision-making as a process, the "grapevine" mode of communication, and such. But only for the most extreme enthusiasts has the newer approach reduced the element of formal organization to impotence.

There is also—as Charles Perrow points out in the *Inter-*

national Encyclopedia of the Social Sciences—a school of sociologists who, looking more broadly at organized human associations, "tend to see formal organizations as complex institutions with evolving goals and a 'character' of their own, rather than as rational instruments designed to pursue a single, rational goal." [1] For example, Philip Selznick in *Leadership in Administration* describes the "formal system of rules and objectives" of an organization that allocates tasks, delegates authority, channels communication, coordinates specialties. He concludes that

> the term "organization" thus suggests a certain bareness, a lean, no-nonsense system of consciously coordinated activities. It refers to an expendable tool, a rational instrument engineered to do a job. An "institution," on the other hand, is more nearly a natural product of social needs and pressures—a responsive, adaptive organism. [2]
>
> [For] an organization is a group of living human beings. The formal or official design for living never completely accounts for what the participants do. It is always supplemented by what is called the "informal structure," which arises as the individual brings into play his own personality, his special problems and interests. Formal relations co-ordinate roles or specialized activities, not persons. Rules apply to foremen and machinists, to clerks, sergeants, and vice-presidents, yet no durable organization is able to hold human experience to these formally defined roles. In actual practice, men tend to interact as many-faceted persons, adjusting to the daily round in ways that spill over the neat boundaries set by their assigned roles.
>
> The formal, technical system is therefore never more than a part of the living enterprise we deal with in action. [3]

The distinction between formal, official organization and the full, living institutional actuality certainly corresponds to commonsense experience and is sociologically useful. But note that the sociologists, like the students of administration, do not absolutize the distinction. They use relativizing phrases such as "tend to" and "more nearly" and "never more than a part of." As Selznick himself points out:

> This distinction is a matter of analysis, not of direct description. It does not mean that any given enterprise must be either one or the other. While an extreme case may closely approach either an "ideal" organization or an "ideal" institution, most living associations resist so easy a classification. They are complex mixtures of both designed and responsive behavior.[4]

Thus it would appear that an institution, although considerably more than a formal organization, is not separate and distinct from its organization but actually involves and includes official organization as one of its dimensions. Institutions are not simply the goal-less, nonrational, undirected aspects of human associations.

The Inevitability of Institutional Commitment

It is particularly relevant for our problem of commitment to notice that, in fact, a prime characteristic of the organization is its possession of a well-defined and shared mission, purpose, or objective. Talcott Parsons, for example, identifies "primacy of orientation to the attainment of a specific goal" as the distinguishing characteristic of organization.[5] Thus the organizational dimension of the institution is the self-conscious locus and bearer not only of the structural and procedural means for achieving ends but also of the official ends themselves. Presumably these announced, explicit goals of the institution typically play a highly influential if not central role in the policy-making and other activities of the institution.

We conclude that the institution, at least in and through its organization, may and typically does declare its adherence to particular doctrines, values, and/or purposes, and pledges itself to policies intended to achieve those purposes. That is, the institution may and does *commit* itself.

Indeed the institutional sociologists hold that, in a certain sense, there are value commitments even in those broader dimensions of the institution beyond the formal organization. According to Selznick, "to institutionalize" is "to infuse with value beyond the technical requirements of the task at hand." [6] An institution tends to become the receptacle of the ideals and values of its individual members, to symbolize the community's aspirations and sense of identity, and thereby to take on certain "character-defining commitments." [7] Its members come to share a common belief and expectation that the whole institution is committed to achieve certain values, which will differ somewhat from the official aims of the organization.

Thus sociologists of whatever school, and whether or not they emphasize the organization-institution distinction, understand goals, values, and norms as constituting a necessary, probably even central and causative, element in the life of an institution. Writing in a standard reference, Louis Schneider finds that the very term "institution" denotes an aspect of social life in which distinctive value orientations and interests, centering upon large and important social concerns (e.g., education, marriage, property), generate or are accompanied by distinctive modes of social interaction.[8] Building his elaboration of this definition on the work of classical sociologists such as Sumner, Hobhouse, MacIver, and Parsons, Schneider concludes that the existence of "value-patterns, norms, standards" (along with interests) is one of the three essential, universal factors in the life of an institution.[9]

The necessity and universality of commitment to purpose in the very existence of institutions seems to require the conclusion that institutions not only may but *must* make and hold to such commitments. If it is true that all institutions must be so committed, both organizationally and humanly, then institutional commitment is not only possible but inevitable.

A pragmatic look at the operational necessities of an institution provides commonsense confirmation of the sociologists' analysis. The institution (whether it be a business corporation, a government agency, a church, a family, a college) is characterized by particular internal structures, processes, and policies. Both at the foundation of the institution and through its ongoing life, human decisions must be made concerning which structures, processes, and policies will be most appropriate and effective. These elements of internal constitution function instrumentally. Rational decision about their effectiveness as means will necessarily depend therefore on the nature of the ends they are intended to serve. These ends are of course the values and goals for whose sake the institution operates, and to which it is committed. Self-conscious commitment to purpose is a functional necessity for every institution.

Clarity of commitment and congruity between instruments and purposes are of course in every actual, particular institution matters of degree. Presumably neither is ever achieved perfectly. But only insofar as purposes are clearly delineated and agreed, and only *insofar as* structures and policies are designed to serve those purposes—only thus far can the institution function coherently and effectively, and its members make decisions rationally. A totally *un*committed institution is a self-contradiction, and not an institution at all.

The Case of the College

Like other institutions, colleges are inevitably committed to particular values and objectives. Their aims are officially stated in their catalogs and their presidents' speeches. Their organizational charts express the usual hierarchy of functional ends and means. Their policies and programs claim to be implementing some coherent and more or less explicit goals. And beyond the official organization there grows in each college community some particular "character" or ethos that is defined by shared value commitments.

More functionally and specifically, decisions about a particular college's policies and programs must be grounded in a shared understanding of its ultimate purposes—if the college is to be a coherent and effective institution. The educational objectives and assumptions of the college must serve as the criteria for the thinking of the faculty and administration as they plan courses and curricula, establish graduation requirements, appraise proposed new programs, recruit faculty and students, set policies for student life, choose modes of teaching, arrange constitutionally the various components of the community, set budgets, evaluate the work of students and the college, and so on. This is why "research into higher education, if it is directed to fundamental problems, soon becomes involved with questions of ends," as Nevitt Sanford has noted.[10]

Indeed, the necessity of self-conscious commitment to well-defined values and purposes would seem to apply with special force to all those institutions whose purpose is *educational*. Schools, colleges, and universities do after all claim that their central objectives concern knowledge and the education of the mind. They must in varying ways and degrees be rational, intellectual communities. They must be able to explain to themselves and to the public their goals, their operating assumptions, their methods.

Perhaps the elementary and secondary schools, on the one hand, and the multiversity, on the other, can get away with leaving their commitments somewhat vague, implicit, and pluralistic. The lower schools operate so integrally with the local culture and teach students so young that their objectives tend to be assumed (unwisely, no doubt) as obvious and exempt from examination. The multiversity escapes or postpones the necessity of explicit and coherent commitment by serving a wide range of social and personal utilitarian needs, and by waving its banner of "freedom to do whatever its members want to do."

The liberal arts college finds it more difficult (though by no means impossible) to leave its commitments vague, ambiguous, implicit, and unexamined. Besides the universal pull of the necessity of operational criteria, there are two special forces at work in the liberal arts college which impel it to become self-aware and articulate about its beliefs, purposes, and assumptions.

First, the aims and processes of liberal education (as distinct from technical and instrumental education) inevitably push its participants toward issues of ethics, philosophy, and theology. Its objective is not simply to instruct students in certain facts and skills but to facilitate the fullest development of human persons. Therefore no philosophic holds are barred, and no ideas can be judged in advance to be irrelevant. Whether in the ferment of particular courses or in debate about the whole curriculum or social policies, argument runs to the frontiers and to the foundations. Faculty, students, and administrators are pressed to articulate and examine critically questions about truly human goals for man and society and about the premises of education itself. The liberal arts college as organization and institution is therefore embarrassed (or ought to be) to whatever extent it is unable to articulate and justify its own objectives and assumptions.

A second and related pressure on the college springs from the fact that, more than with other types of institutions, questions of purpose and commitment must be the concern of the *whole* community—specifically including the students. For varying reasons, perhaps only the leaders and policy-makers of business corporations, government agencies, elementary schools, and multiversities need to understand deeply the purposes and presuppositions to which the institution is committed. But it is essential to the effective operation of a college of liberal learning that the college's perception of its mission be widely shared, and that the maximum proportion of faculty and students be involved in thinking critically about the philosophy of their educational enterprise and its implementation. The liberal arts college rightly urges its students to analyze deeply and to commit themselves to the values they find authentic, but it had better be prepared for the consequences of this urging on its own life. Indeed it should want to be: there is evidence that the colleges that are clearest and most serious about their own commitments have the greatest educational impact on their students, as Philip Jacob has shown in *Changing Values in College*.[11]

Perhaps for some institutions, under some conditions, purposes and presuppositions are best left implicit and unquestioned. The contemporary liberal arts college is not one of these. Its value commitments and operating assumptions must be made explicit and publicly promulgated —so that the whole community may understand and cooperate in implementing them, and also so that they may be deliberately examined and criticized. As Morris Keeton and Conrad Hilberry make clear:

> Every university or college exhibits, at least implicitly, a philosophy and a purpose. These contain within them strong value-commitments that have a powerful impact on what is learned, for they are the pervasive atmosphere of the place. They are, if not made explicit, the things most likely to be learned as unquestioned, therefore the things most likely to be illiberally learned, learned in an intellectually unsound way. . . . It is essential to the best doubting of purposes to be clear as to what institutional purpose really is.[12]

Our analysis suggests that, like other institutions, only more so, the liberal arts college has no choice but to be committed to some purpose or other, and to some particular set of operating assumptions. Its only choices concern the substance of its commitments, and the way in which they are held and expressed. The substance must be left to each college. But our brief review does imply certain guidelines for the mode and status of college commitment:

1. The educational purposes and operating presuppositions of the college ought to be coherent and clear.
2. These commitments ought to be expressed explicitly and publicly to the whole community.
3. These commitments ought to serve as the operating

criteria for all the policies and programs of the college, as ends to means.

4. These commitments ought to be open to continuous critical reappraisal by members of the community.

One of the exciting issues left open by this line of analysis is the question of the philosophic "level" of the college's commitments. We have spoken of commitment to particular "educational values, purposes and assumptions"— implying criteria that are primarily ethical and at a certain level of abstraction. Can and ought the college's commitments be left at this proximate level—or must they be concerned with the more nearly ultimate logical *grounds* of its values and presuppositions? Must or ought a college commit itself, not only to certain ethical-educational criteria, but to particular understandings of human nature and destiny, ultimate value and reality?

The direction and momentum of our present argument make it difficult to stop short, and beg the ultimate questions. Surely the advertised claim of some colleges to aim simply for educational quality or excellence is transparently empty. The somewhat more sophisticated commitment to humane values still yields few if any usable criteria, unless it is filled in with substance. To which conception of human nature—the Greek, the Biblical, the fascist—does one turn to discover the substance of humane values? A college's judgment about what values are authentically humane and what operating assumptions are realistic must be grounded logically in at least some particular image of *man*. Kenneth Hansen has written in *Philosophy for American Education*:

For every educational system of any sort has as its primary aim doing something with and about man and the

children of men. Perhaps the educational system seeks
to train their minds, to make them better citizens, to
build moral character, to direct learning experiences, to
provide for individual and social growth—but whatever
the aim or aims, and on whatever assumptions these educational aims may be based, the common denominator of
concern of all systems of education is with man. . . . The
question "what is man?" may be rephrased to ask "whom
do we educate?" or "what does education do for human
beings?" This question, however phrased, is central
both to the philosophy and to the practice of education.[13]

Are liberal arts colleges today able to articulate clearly the
substance and foundations of their educational purposes
and operating assumptions? It would be difficult to docu-
ment a challenge to the accuracy of Nevitt Sanford's negative appraisal:

The inarticulateness of these colleges about their aims is
often baffling, and so is their failure to understand the
real sources of their difficulties. In many of these colleges
there is a grave concern about such problems as raising
standards and getting students to work harder. Generally speaking, the liberal arts colleges are certainly trying
to do *something*. It is remarkable, as Santayana noted,
how we redouble our efforts as we lose sight of our
goals.[14]

CHAPTER 3

The Sectarian Nature
of Liberal Education

EDITOR'S INTRODUCTION

Are religious and moral commitments superadded to a college of the liberal arts and sciences? Do they represent an alien and therefore undue burden which inevitably distracts the college from its proper educational mission? Editor Lloyd Averill holds that, both historically and philosophically, religious and moral questions are what liberal education is all about. He insists that *educational* integrity requires that a liberal arts college commit itself, at least provisionally, to some answers about the human condition, which is the point where the religious and the moral converge most acutely.

Lloyd J. Averill is Dean of the Faculty and Professor of Religion and Sociology in Davis and Elkins College.

Lloyd J. Averill

The Sectarian Nature
of Liberal Education

If the church-related college displays a marked uncertainty about its identity these days, it comes by that uncertainty honestly. On the one hand, it is being moved by our theologians of the secular, and seconded by the church board secretaries who follow them, that since religion is dubious as a substantive category, the college will do better simply to address itself to what are thought to be exclusively educational issues. On the other hand, the college finds itself scarcely the master of its own destiny in any case, pushed as it is by professional organizations and pressed by graduate schools, and faced as it is by competition from secular institutions, both public and private. To make matters worse, many church-related institutions believe that their own survival will depend upon claiming an increasing portion of the federal tax dollar, and it is by no means clear how church relation may affect their future eligibility for public funds.

The problem with past discussions of the Christian college's identity, and perhaps the reason as well why the colleges have been so defensive and the discussion relatively

Reprinted, in revised form, from "Education to Enhance the Human," *The Christian Century*, October 9, 1968. Used by permission.

fruitless, is that it has sought a misplaced uniqueness. The Christian college has assumed that if it took its religious as well as its educational intent seriously, it would find itself occupying some kind of educational ghetto. I want to insist, on the contrary, that the Christian college is only a special instance of a community of educational concern which is at least as broad as the liberal arts tradition, that the religious question is precisely integral to that tradition, under whatever auspices, and that failure to face the religious question subverts the tradition itself.

If the Christian college is a special instance of a general class, that does not diminish the significance of what distinguishes it from others in the class. And if liberal arts colleges of secular predilection have failed to come clean on the religious issues resident within their liberal profession, then they should be invited to do so.

One critic—a denominational executive—has charged that concern for religion has turned the Christian college into a "quasi-religious institution." My contention is that failure to take the religious questions seriously will turn any liberal arts college into a "quasi-educational" institution. What follows is an attempt to give substance to this analysis of the issue.

I

President John Sloan Dickey, of Dartmouth College, has accurately observed that the American liberal arts college, whether church-related or not, has had a "unique mission in the duality of its historic purpose: to see men made whole in both competence and conscience." [1] In this the American colleges were following the example of their academic prototype, the English university college, where moral learning was seen as the necessary complement to intellectual development. A century ago William Cory, master of Eton, wrote:

> You go to a great school, not for knowledge so much as for arts and habits; for the habit of attention, for the art of expression, for the art of assuming at a moment's notice a new intellectual posture, for the art of entering quickly into another person's thoughts, for the habit of submitting to censure and refutation, for the art of indicating assent or dissent in graduated terms, for the habit of regarding minute points of accuracy, for the habit of working out what is possible in a given time, for taste, for discrimination, for mental courage and mental soberness. Above all, you go to a great school for self-knowledge.

Still today at Oxford each student is assigned to a moral tutor as well as to an academic tutor, and at Cambridge the undergraduate's college supervisor is expected to concern himself with the total development of his student and not alone with his academic development.

If the American college derived its immediate model from the English educational experience, this view of the aim of education has a far broader heritage. In commenting on William Cory's description cited above, George Stern, of Syracuse University, has remarked:

> Cory's words sound contemporary, but they would have seemed so to Socrates as well. Although he wrote them in the 1860's, the education for which he speaks has been coterminous with Western civilization. Now, on the threshhold of their decline, the need for preserving such exercises in the development of wisdom has never been greater.[2]

II

If Cory's words sound contemporary, that is because they are reconfirmed in much contemporary educational philosophy. The most persistent theme in current definitions of liberal education emphasizes its humanizing intent: the whole person is the subject and personal wholeness is the end. Matter is not to be considered in isolation from meaning, nor the mental in isolation from the moral. All are integral to the process within which a man is increasingly freed to become fully a man. Elsewhere I have essayed the task of definition in these terms:

> Liberal education is intended to serve genuinely humanizing ends. For this reason, educational concern is directed toward the student as a person rather than as a function. The college seeks to enable him to become a more complete man and not just a more efficient technician. . . . In the presence of cultural and academic forces which tend toward the fragmentation of knowledge, the liberal arts college seeks to foster an awareness of the interdependence and the complementarity of the several intellectual methods and disciplines, and it does this as a means of inculcating intellectual humility and intellectual wholeness in student and teacher alike.[3]

That this is no merely idiosyncratic definition is clear from a variety of other witnesses. Provost Gerhard Spiegler, of Haverford College, has written that

> the aim of the liberal arts education is to make men more fully human. The whole man is to be educated and human wholeness is the end of liberal education. The health of man is to be achieved by deepening the hu-

manity of man. The liberally educated man is the
healthy man.[4]

Dr. E. J. Shoben, formerly of the American Council on
Education, has properly reminded us that "the liberal arts
are not subjects in the curriculum. Rather, they are personal qualities—the attributes of men that enlarge their
capacity for uncoerced choice." [5] And Professors Fred
Newmann and Donald Oliver, of Harvard, assert that "the
most fundamental objective of education is the development of human dignity, or self-realization within community." [6]

Colleges which are currently attempting a radical return
to the root meaning of liberal education have done so
precisely at this point. So Professor Erlend Jacobsen recently wrote that Goddard College is "dedicated to the
notion that education is primarily the reconstruction of
one's own experience for oneself." [7] And Dean Arthur
Borden, of New College (Florida), wrote:

> There is a place in the educational world for the small
> liberal arts college. That place is not primarily to train
> for an occupation or to prepare for graduate school, but
> to provide a liberal education by giving students the
> opportunity to experience education as a process of
> realizing their own potential and by emphasizing the
> interrelationship of all knowledge. . . . [New College]
> further adheres to the principle that the students' life on
> campus outside the classroom is an important part of
> their educational experience.[8]

Indeed, the typically residential character of the liberal
arts college is not simply an arrangement of convenience
but is as well the persistent and tangible manifestation of

the comprehensive life-context within which liberal learning takes place.

Without irresponsible oversimplification, therefore, *the liberal arts college past and present can be described as an educational strategy for enhancing the human.* The conclusion of such a line of argument is this: efforts are misplaced which attempt to locate the uniqueness of the church-related college in its professed humanistic intent— its concern for the moral as well as the mental, for the meaning of experience as well as the structure of experience. These are not the unique contribution of the Christian tradition to education; they are, on the contrary, generic to the liberal tradition in education under whatever auspices.

III

This affirmation of humanistic intent which is generic to the liberal credo in education has inevitable consequence for the shape of the college's curricular arrangement. Professor Spiegler has asserted perceptively that "the curriculum of a liberal arts college is a complex value judgment. The liberal arts college, if it purports to inculcate values must itself embrace values; it must commit itself." [9] It must, indeed, commit itself to develop a curriculum which will enhance the human.

This affirmation similarly has consequences for the shape of the academic community as a community. Professors Newmann and Oliver insist quite correctly that "however one defines dignity or fulfillment, the nature of the society within which it develops is critical." [10] In support of this contention, they cite the comments of G. Kateb in a recent issue of *Daedalus*:

Selves to be realized are given their essential qualities by their societies, and . . . the process of self-realization is a process of continuous involvement with society, as society not only shapes but employs everyone's inner riches. *The upshot is that thought about possible styles of life or about the nature of man is necessary to give sense to the idea of individuality. Far from being an oppressive encroachment, social theory . . . is a basic duty.*[11]

Newmann and Oliver conclude, therefore, that

educational policy should be based on deliberation and inquiry into the needs of the individual within community. Every educator faithful to this premise should be able, therefore, to explicate and clarify the particular conception of society or community upon which he justifies his educational recommendations.[12]

Thus the shape of the liberal academic community as community can be justified only to the degree that it enhances the human.

Institutional engagement in the questions of the nature of man and society, and institutional commitment to some answers, however provisional, to these questions, is absolutely essential if there is to be any integrity between a college's profession of its humanistic intent and the actual process of education which goes on there. It is important to emphasize again that what I have been describing above, with aid of my citations, is not alone the church-related liberal arts college but *any* institution of higher learning which stands within the liberal tradition.

The nature of the person and of the interpersonal is not, however, normatively and self-evidently given to an objective examination of historical experience. Understandings of the human vary and vie with one another. They distinguish the major philosophical systems and practical social strategies throughout the long reflective history of man. Democratic naturalism and Marxist materialism, Christianity and Buddhism, socialism and capitalism, Fascism and anarchism: each embodies a distinctive set of beliefs about man and society which sets it apart from the others. Each represents a long tradition of experience and critical reflection. Sporadic attempts to create an artificial synthesis of such world views seem historically irrepressible but inevitably destined for failure in spite of their undoubted good intentions. A world view is not, after all, an arbitrary or synthetic construct. Each is a lived response to life which catches up a funded experience of profound historical range and human depth which for that very reason defies conflation. This is not to say that each of these historic traditions views man and society in monolithic terms, though they may sometimes give that appearance to outsiders. There is, for example, no wholly univocal Christian doctrine of man, though all Christian views bear the marks of a common kinship; and we are learning something of the varied shapes Marxism can take.

This, then, is the context within which a college's engagement with the questions of the nature of man and society must take place. It is a context which is not just incidentally religious and moral; it is inherently religious and moral. To ask what it may mean to enhance the human is to locate oneself at precisely the point where the religious and the moral converge most acutely. The conclusion, in my view, is inescapable: the liberal arts college which intends to be educationally serious will also be religiously and morally serious. And to be serious will mean to commit itself to some answers, however provisional, to these questions—answers which can shape its curriculum and its style of life so that the human is enhanced. *Then to be a liberal arts college at all means to be "sectarian," at least in this sense, that some meanings of the human and the humane are embraced while others are rejected.*

Some educational institutions take the view that, *qua* institution, such a commitment is inappropriate and must be left to individual administrators, teachers, and students. The more obvious thing to be said about such a view is that it is, in itself, a commitment which, like other forms of commitment, excludes certain options even while it endorses others. The less obvious thing to be said about such a view is that it is self-deceptive; for since, as we have already seen, the curriculum is a complex value judgment, to have a curriculum at all is to have institutionalized a majority value consensus and given it a certain authority over the institution's members. Thus the institution which professes to eschew institutional commitment finds itself in the unhappy condition of professing neutrality while taking sides.

IV

In the terms of this argument, then, in the American society a church-related liberal arts college is distinguished from other liberal arts colleges primarily at two points:

1. It is distinctive in its self-conscious relationship to a distinctive institutional subculture within the larger society, that subculture being the organized Christian community. A liberal arts college whose spiritual roots lie in a philosophic humanism may be conscious of its place in a long and distinguished tradition reaching as far back as the pre-Socratics, but that tradition has no contemporary insti-

tutional manifestation comparable to the Christian church. This means that the church-related college locates itself as a part of a larger institutionalized social movement, which larger movement is concerned with other activities as well as with education. This self-conscious relationship of the college to the Christian community does not necessarily imply control of the college by that community, though in special instances such control does exist. I would argue that where it exists, it is a purely prudential institutional arrangement which is required neither by the nature of the institutional church nor—as the entire argument above is intended to demonstrate—by the fact that the college locates itself within a Christian world view. Where, as in very many Protestant-related colleges, no church control or even substantial church influence over college policy exists, the church-relatedness of the college lies partly in its desire to identify itself with the servant mission of the larger Christian enterprise and to do so within its own integrity as a community of unrestricted inquiry.

2. It is distinctive in its commitment to a Christian view of man and society and its determination to translate that commitment into curriculum and life-style. Precisely what that means, theologically, may vary as widely as the theological enterprise itself has varied historically. Surely a considerable consensus would cluster around two affirmations. One is that the distinctive *humanum* of man is located in the fact that he is man-in-relation-to-God. This means, to use Tillich's language, a rejection of autonomous man (who determines his own meaning and shapes his own nature by the exertion of his own will) and of heteronomous man (who is determined and shaped by the imposition of an alien, external institutional will). The other is that what it means to be man-in-relation-to-God is given

normatively in Jesus Christ. Because of prevailing mis-
conceptions within the community of higher education
itself, it is important again to emphasize that such commitment is not something which is added to, or essentially
different from, the college's educational purpose. On the
contrary, to be a responsible liberal arts college intent upon
enhancing the human, it must possess some clarity and conviction about the nature of the human that is to be enhanced.

*Thus for the Christian college, its educational intent is
precisely its religious intent, and its religious intent is precisely its educational intent.*

CHAPTER 4

The Identity
of the Christian College

EDITOR'S INTRODUCTION

Is it true, as some have asserted, that a Christian college is theocentric, whereas a secular college is anthropocentric? Editor William Jellema thinks not. Both colleges are concerned with man; they differ in their views of who man is. But that does not mean that the distinctiveness of the Christian commitment in higher education is limited to contributing its peculiar view of the human, though that is where the previous essay left the matter. Jellema thinks there is more at issue. The very concept of human *wholeness* itself, he argues, comes primarily from Biblical anthropology rather than from Greek thought. Colleges in other traditions may use the language of wholeness, but they lack an ideological heritage with which to make the most of it. And the unity of the human, as the Bible affirms it, has important implication as well for that other major preoccupation of liberal learning, the unity of human knowledge.

William W. Jellema is Executive Associate and Research Director in the Association of American Colleges.

William W. Jellema

The Identity
of the Christian College

THE CHRISTIAN* COLLEGE IN THIS CENTURY IS BEING FORCED
to examine itself and its *raison d'être* for the first time in
its history. The first American colleges were established
to provide society with a natively educated ministry. A
building or two and ministers made a college. There was
no felt need for a "philosophy" of education beyond this.
Some agency had to nurture learning in order that the
church not be crippled by ignorant ministers. It was as
simple as that.

Unlike the immigrant, who has to come to a strange
country to discover that he is different, the christian college,
more like the American Indian, discovered its difference
not by moving but by perceiving its changed environment.
Looking at its environment in the second half of the
twentieth century, the christian college discovers that it is
   —relatively small, in a society that does not prize small-
      ness as a virtue;
   —a liberal arts college, when that concept of education is
      fighting for its life and identity;

---

* The adjective "christian," when capitalized, is either privileged or
pejorative. The lower case *c* is used here in an attempt to invite a critical
reading on the part of those disposed to react favorably to the word and
a fair hearing on the part of those conditioned to respond to it negatively.

—purportedly christian, when both society and the church have become avowedly secular;

—undergraduate, when prestige in academe has passed to graduate education;

—often rural, when the populace and its problems are clearly urban;

—emphasizing teaching, when professional status is achieved through research and publication.

Not only that, but ministers have long since been prepared in separate professional schools called theological seminaries.

The identity crisis hitting the christian college is neither unique nor necessarily alarming. Negro colleges, women's colleges, junior colleges, and former teachers colleges are all confronted with identity crises. This is healthy. A periodic challenge to identity is a most useful occasion for reexamining and reinterpreting goals and purposes and for bringing about change. The crisis is alarming only when it is met with the mindless assumption that fidelity to purpose forbids change. What René Dubos wrote about the individual applies with equal force to the institution.

To live is to struggle. A successful life is one during which . . . an adequate number of effective responses have been made to the constant challenges of . . . physical and social environment.[1]

The institution, like the man, may yearn for an earlier and simpler era when the categories seemed clearer and it could be sure of its identity, but the adventure of human history denies fulfillment of this yearning.

I

The christian college is an institution. That is where the difficulty begins. The rate of specious reactions to the institutional noticeably increases when you place modifiers like "christian" before the word "college," but the problem really begins with the fact that the college is an institution, and the institutional is in disrepute among us.

While I am not yet ready to join Herbert Stroup, of Brooklyn College, in a defense of bureaucracy in education, I am ready to begin a defense of its institutionalization.

An institution is a social creation, a combination—perhaps a compromise—of the vision of more than one person. It is the concrete expression of an ideal and a commitment. However, we are no longer idealists, nor do we make commitments. This is true not only of our response to large institutions—the state, the church, the college—but of our response to smaller ones as well—the family—and even to ourselves as continuing persons.

We and our students are non- or anti-ideological, and our commitments are primarily to our selves-of-the-moment. When our commitments are broader they are too existential (not to say too ephemeral) to be institutionalized. In a brilliant paper Kenneth Keniston said:

All of these new types [of students] . . . are essentially privatistic. . . . Even for the student activist, the main tension is not the effort to realize a vision of social reform, but the tension between his private search for meaning and his public activities. To attribute this tension solely to the bureaucratization, impersonality, and bigness of the university is an oversimplification and an evasion. For the university only reflects the characteristics of American society. . . . His [the activist's] commitment is not a commitment to a way of life or to a coherent set of political beliefs; rather it is "existential" in its emphasis on simple personal expressions or moral indignation.[2]

Why are we anti-institutional? Part of the reason may be the ongoing struggle of form with substance, not new on the contemporary scene. Part of the reason is our ready acceptance of change and our suspicion of resistance to it. Keniston says we are privatists. And we are privatists both because public life calls for competence (and blandness), as Keniston indicates, but also because of our selfishness and limited vision.

But why are Christians anti-institutionalists? Some of them answer: because the institutional is the demonic. The letter replaces the spirit. The institution perpetuates itself long after the ideal it was created to serve is lost. What was a humble means becomes a pompous self-serving end.

Clearly, the institutional can become demonic. But this tendency does not sufficiently justify the anti-institutional attitude. Nor does apprehension over this tendency adequately explain the phenomenon of anti-institutionalism.

Others argue that the times demand an anti-institutional attitude. We live in a time of such accelerated change that men like Harvey Cox have called for a "theology of revolution." A permanently unsettled and fluid state seems to be the christian ideal. However, the roots of the anti-institutional attitude are not in our time. They have a deeper history.

One of the earliest philosophical modes to be rejected by christianity as heretical stemmed from an attempt to reconcile with christian thought a philosophical notion that radically separated the material world, which was considered evil, from the spiritual world, which was considered good. These reconcilers were called Docetists from the Greek word *dokeo* meaning "seem" or "think." It only "seemed" that Christ had a real body, they said, for the spiritual world cannot really become incarnate in the material world.

This docetic attitude continues to trouble us. Many of us encounter real problems with the notion of incarnation: not only with the incarnation of the Word, but with the incarnate expressions of ideals in our friends—how do you reconcile the ordinariness of their lives with the ideals they profess?—and with the incarnation of our corporate ideals in an institution. We want truth, love, and justice without messy, defiling incarnations.

I mentioned this idea in a recent exchange of correspondence with a former colleague at the University of Michigan, Stephen Tonsor, a professor of history. He responded:

> The theme of incarnationalism and secularity (in the best, Christian sense of that word) are terribly important in our reviving the Christian colleges. We must not be afraid of the muck and grime of everyday men and the everyday world. . . . Nor must Christian colleges be afraid of failure and of ideals corrupted. That is part of everyday life.

To this I add only that we have a heretical conception of the meaning of the word "christian" that keeps us from applying it as freely as it deserves. We often hesitate to use it because we think that this designates some pious spiritual perfection—and this is why the corruption and failure of christian persons and institutions so severely upset us. But this is not what the word designates. It designates commitment and intent. Institutions do not often fulfill the ideals we romantically hold for them. But neither are they unrelievedly evil. As Kenneth Underwood perceived, they are "ambiguous human creations offering the possibility of carrying out . . . personal and corporate acts." [3] A godlike person or institution you can neither be nor create. A christian one you can.

II

The christian college has heard often enough that to achieve identity it must be unique. One of Manning Pattillo and Donald MacKenzie's recommendations in the Danforth study was that the church-related college be experimental and different. Earlier, in 1961, Earl McGrath, addressing the Council of Protestant Colleges and Universities, said:

> A reaffirmation of an institution's religious affiliation and the consequent shaping of its entire life in accordance with its declared religious purpose will give new meaning and clearer features to its program. . . . Until these colleges clearly reestablish their peculiar mission they will have no *unique* service to perform. In the intensifying competition, without a unique service, they will not be able to survive as church-related liberal arts colleges.

Even distinctive characteristics, however, let alone uniqueness, are hard to discover in the church-related college. In the apt language of an observer not in the West, they often appear to be merely institutions of "pious secularism." They are imitative and the most well off are the most imitative. And when they imitate, they imitate the secular institutions. They take their notions about what constitutes education and educational programming from other institutions whose major virtue may be that they do not profess a uniqueness they do not possess.

One reason why they may not be unique in program is that experimentation is expensive and failure is extremely costly. Only the Ford Motor Company can afford an Edsel. (And then only if they can recoup with a Mustang.)

But the larger reason why christian colleges are imitative may be the problem of discovering the line that connects the determination to be a christian college with the uniqueness of the program it should offer.

The problem with seeking identity as a christian college is that the decision to be "christian" does not automatically dictate the ways in which the college should try to be unique. It may be both desirable and necessary for institutions to specialize, but the college that elects to identify itself as christian does not simultaneously receive a revelation of the ways in which one should be different or the areas to emphasize for distinction.

The christian interest is a catholic interest. *Nothing* is disqualified from its interest. Specialization must be chosen on other bases. After one has chosen the areas of specialization, however, the decision to pursue these as a christian institution may suggest modifications and enrichments.

I suggest that the christian liberal arts college has at least three special opportunities to be distinctive, perhaps unique, and certainly useful:

1. To the rest of higher education, offering christian insights into the nature of the objects of study;
2. To its students, cooperating with them in the search for an integrative whole;
3. To the church, demonstrating its concern for higher education and carrying on research and writing concerning the mutual implications that learning and faith have for each other.

III

One of the distinctive emphases that a christian scholar can bring to higher education is some insights of the faith. Since a view of the nature of man lies at the foundation of education, let me examine *a* christian view for its insights and relevance.

W. H. Cowley once sought to establish a distinction that would have granted the nonchurch-related institution a corner on man. "The term secularism," he wrote, ". . . does not fairly designate non-church-related colleges and universities since to many people it unjustifiably connotes materialism and hedonism. A better term would be *anthropocentrism.*" Church-related colleges, he added, are, by definition, theocentric.[4]

I do not agree.

George A. Buttrick tells a memorable story about two men who walked down the stairs of a building in the garment district. One of them flicked a cigaret into a pail of water on the landing—except that it was naphtha and not water. When the naphtha exploded, one man ran down the stairs to the street; the other ran upstairs to warn the women working there of the fire. Both men, acknowledges Buttrick, were intent on self-preservation: the difference lay in their conception of the self. Likewise, the difference between the christian college and the avowedly secular institution does not lie in the fact that one attends to God whereas the other attends to man. Both, as educational institutions, are concerned with man. A possible difference lies in their understanding of who man is.

Perhaps the first thing to be said about the christian view of man is that he is a whole man. Others have affirmed this also, but it deserves iteration that the concept of the wholeness of man is primarily a Biblical and christian contribution to an understanding of his nature. It is a heritage of Greek thought to conceive of man as composed of parts: an immortal soul, a spark of the divine nature itself, undying, immortal; and a material shell, a body, mortal, diseased, perhaps sinful, and dying. In this conception (also, unhappily, a popular christian view) the body is a prison in which the immortal soul is incarcerated. The idea of salvation is to separate this unlikely and unpleasant combination: to "get the angel out of the slot machine," as it were. At death the body returns to the miserable stuff of which it is made, and the soul returns to the Great Soul of which it is a part.

The Biblical view knows nothing of man as composed of parts, whether body, soul, or any other. Man is a whole man. He is not an incarnate soul but an animated body. The Bible knows nothing of such a term as "immortal soul," as the Greeks knew nothing of such a term as "the mind of the flesh."

Because man is seen to be a whole man does not necessarily mean that the college must attend to all facets of his being and give them equal weight. It does mean that it cannot conduct its operations in such a way as to suggest that man is not a whole being. The sterile atmosphere of many an institution of higher learning that treats the life of the mind as though it can be divorced from the rest of man who lives in the "real" world has deservedly earned the active hostility of its students. When departments perform the acrobatics of their discipline over a net the students are scornful, and rightly so. The man who can think conceptually is the same man who feels and wills and acts. The man who needs to know needs also to believe; and, in the words of former President Pusey, of

Harvard, "What we want especially to do is to believe knowingly and to know with conviction." [5]   Man is a whole man.

Christian insight into the nature of man adds a unique dimension which is expressed through the concept of the *imago Dei*. The notion that man bears the image of God has often been interpreted to mean that he is capable of rational thought. The Greeks admired a man's reason above all other faculties and assigned it a primacy of rank and function. It is not difficult to see why they did so. Nor is it difficult to see why christian thinkers have associated the *imago Dei* with man's rational capacity.

However, I understand the *imago* to be that God-given capacity and freedom in man to reflect and pattern himself after the value structure, God, or gods to which he commits himself. Fallen man may have lost the *imago Dei*, but he has not lost the *imago* capacity. He can reflect his own self, he can reflect a more cosmopolitan humanity, or he can reflect the God of Abraham, Isaac, and Jacob. It is the *imago* capacity that gives man his real uniqueness as man. It is the *imago* freedom that is his first—and, perhaps, his only—freedom. He can choose what god he will serve and by what final conviction and purpose he shall live. Ultimately, the only true freedom is religious freedom.

Man is not only capable of commitment, of passionate devotion to an ideal; he is so made that he *must* mirror his ultimate convictions. Even shirking commitment demands decision. Man's glory as well as his tragedy is that he is capable of making commitments that are total. When he commits himself, he commits the whole man.

The concept of the image implies for education that the student should be given opportunity to reflect on the One in whose image he was created, and to consider the One in whom that image was most perfectly made manifest.

But it means further that he must be treated in such a way that he can make a commitment that is authentic, freely made, and made in the presence of an intelligent understanding of live alternatives. The fact that man is a commitment-making being means that a student does not arrive at college without commitments; nor can his commitment-making be arrested while there; nor can he mature in his ability to make wise and considered commitments by being restricted from opportunity to exercise this freedom.

IV

One of the visions of the liberal arts college has been that of the unity of knowledge. This vision is attributable certainly as much to the Greeks with their philosophical concept that things were one at bottom as to any christian certainty that all truth ultimately emanates from God. It owes something too to the Greek passion for ordering, arranging, and systematizing. But the christian conception of all creation joined together under God likewise contributes to this vision. It is not *peculiarly* christian to be disconcerted by the fragmentation of knowledge and by the antiseptic separation of learning from living, but these additional insights provide the christian college with special impetus and opportunity to seek distinction in pursuing, with its students, the integration of life and knowledge. The concept of the wholeness of man, moreover, implies that what is taught ought to recall his wholeness and not further fragment him.

This is what Kenneth Underwood's study as summarized in the publication *New Wine* is about: "relating moral and affectional dimensions of learning to the bodies of knowledge for effective responsible action in the world." The relation between ethical inquiry and technical insight must be consciously pursued in the christian college. As William Kolb says elsewhere in *New Wine*, "Knowledge will not fully perform its historic function unless it is integrated into the deeds of moral agents acting in the social arena." [6]

The consequences of fragmented education have often been noted. "Where there is little concerted effort to see life whole," said Walter Moberly, "students are unconsciously conditioned to irresponsibility for its conduct." [7] What is needed, said Kenneth Keniston, is "an education and an environment that encourages students to gather intellect, ethical sense, and action into one related whole." [8]

One of the factors perpetuating the fragmentation of knowledge is the exclusion of theology from serious study and interaction with other fields. From a monopoly, theology proceeded to a position of primacy, from primacy to equality, from equality to bare toleration, and then to exclusion. The effort to aid students to achieve a sense of the wholeness of knowledge is severely limited on any campus where they must proceed in virtual ignorance of this area. This need not be the case at the christian college.

There, theology can be important: perhaps still reign as queen of the sciences. But it must be integrative theology. Theology is an amorous queen: embracing, wooing, and being wooed. Or, to choose another image, theology is not the sole lookout in the crow's nest. Theology is a sentry who sees well the terrain before him but whose contribution to the security of the fortress is shared with other sentries stationed at other vantage points whose views and perspectives are equally important for the strength of the camp.

What students may be looking for is some sort of "running reconciliation" of learning and the faith. Paraphrasing Whitehead, they may be seeking "a [theologically]

imaginative consideration of learning." The inadequacy
of a literal interpretation of the Genesis account as an integrative statement relating the faith to a scientific world
view is less irritating than the absence of an integrative
statement workable for today. One can live with a statement that will need to be changed, perhaps radically. It
is vexing to have to live without one altogether—or with
one forged either by a mind working in isolation from
theology or by a theological mind working in isolation
from science.

To develop such statements of integration the christian
college must offer a broader freedom and commitment than
that afforded under the AAC-AAUP statement on academic freedom which restricts freedom to the discipline.
Integration cannot be pursued where a man may not venture beyond the confines of his discipline. The scholar,
like Martin Luther, makes claim to freedom in the name
of his more fundamental allegiance and dedication. He
accepts rather than claims his christian freedom, and with
it he acknowledges his human finitude, accepts responsibility for the stewardship of his abilities, and recognizes
his responsibility for love and honesty toward people as
well as toward subject matter.

V

The christian college, finally, has special opportunity with
regard to the church, not only as the church's demonstration
of its concern for higher education, but as its closest resource for social criticism and as its primary locus for carrying on research and analysis that relates the advances of
learning to the christian faith. These could be the college's
very special tasks, and ones that it has little fulfilled.

Many institutions of higher learning serve functions besides the teaching of undergraduates. Yet I doubt if any church-related college or its constituency has considered seriously enough that the church-related college ought to be supported as more than a place where the undergraduate is educated. It ought to be supported as a place where the thought of the church goes on, exploring relationships of learning and faith for the christian community and as a place where the social criticism and action of the church is explored and developed. This exploration is not being done in the theological seminary where a limited band handle the responsibilities of a professional school. Nor is it being done in denominational boards, nor in the pulpit. It is not being done.

Whether the church needs several centers to do this or one institute is a separate question. It is sufficient in this context to point out that this is a very useful function which a college might well undertake to perform in the absence of such performance by any other agency. It is a task congruent with its purpose as an educational institution.

To recapitulate: It is quite legitimate to think of a christian institution. Followers of a God who incarnated his Word need not shy away from incarnating their best thinking. But the college's contribution may be less a uniqueness than an opportunity for special emphases and special service: to the rest of higher education, to its students, to the church. These opportunities, needs, and emphases may change. The christian college sets a pattern —and prepares for the end of its separate existence when a new and purer age of Constantine may be ushered in and society adopt for its own those peculiar emphases which have been the contribution of the christian college.

Part II
COMMITMENTS
AND THE DIMENSIONS
OF LEARNING

CHAPTER 5

Discursive Truth
and Evangelical Truth

EDITOR'S INTRODUCTION

"Colleges and universities exist for the pursuit of truth." That
is probably the most commonly heard statement of educational
mission, within the academic community as well as outside of
it. And it is unexceptionable as far as it goes. The difficulty
is that it does not go far enough. Those who assert that slogan
seem to hold, simplemindedly, that the concept of "truth" is
univocal, meaning exclusively "that which can be verified by
discursive or scientific means." On that definition, a college
may legitimately leave quite out of account such nonverifiable
matters as belief and value; it may inquire into matter but not
into meaning. Albert Outler insists, on the contrary, that there
are *two* dimensions to truth, not just one, and that each dimension needs the other for its own full truthfulness. "Truth about
structure" and "truth about meaning" belong together within
the purview of higher education. Only when *both* are fully

affirmed can it finally be said that "colleges and universities exist for the pursuit of truth."

Albert C. Outler is Professor of Theology in the Perkins School of Theology, Southern Methodist University.

Albert C. Outler

Discursive Truth
and Evangelical Truth

IT IS TRAGIC THAT MANY MEN HAVE FELT THAT THEY HAD TO choose between a Christian anti-intellectualism and an anti-Christian intellectualism, between the savants and the saints. It is a great pity that so few have steadfastly maintained that sort of Christian intellectualism which can be genuinely humane without being a whit less faithful to evangelical truth.

But what is truth? Here we come to the heart of the matter and yet most of us feel a deep uneasiness when we try to face it. Truth is a prime academic virtue. The word appears in our mottoes and pronouncements, and no one speaks against it. George Williams has told the story of the famous row over the motto on the Harvard seal—

Abridged from *Quid Est Veritas*, an address delivered at the first annual meeting of the Council of Protestant Colleges and Universities, and published by the Council. Reprinted by permission of Albert C. Outler.

whether it should be *in Christi gloriam, Christus et Ecclesiae*, or simply, *Veritas*. As we know *Veritas* triumphed—but what did it mean? Actually, at Harvard in the mid-nineteenth century and since (and elsewhere) *veritas* meant *discursive* truth, the sort of truth that can be discovered and verified by discursive imagination, analysis, and thought, whether in the closed systems of mathematics and logic or in the imaginative and constructive processes of experimental science, the humanities, and the fine arts. Truth, in this sense, is either the relationship between human judgment and empirical fact or else the end product of rational consent or social consensus. Truth is what is known or knowable about the world and human experience by means of our comprehension of the intelligible patterns and structures and values in the world and in our experience. In the nature of the case, discursive truth is pluralistic, ranging from the relatively simple procedures of gap-filling (a number series, a syllogism, or a fugue) to quite complex imaginal construction (e.g., cosmology, sociology, and metaphysics). Truth, in this sense, is what Plato and Aristotle meant by truth, what the Renaissance meant by truth, what the Enlightenment meant by truth, what the vast majority of modern intellectuals mean by *Veritas*.

Yet this is *not* what the New Testament means by the term *aletheia*—the historical "source" of the term in the Harvard motto. The word *aletheia* occurs almost a hundred times in the New Testament, and it *never* means discursive truth. Instead, its consistent denotation is to the reality of God, "naturally" concealed in the Mystery of Being but now "unconcealed" in the Mystery of Redemption. *A-letheia* means, quite literally, "without a *lethon*" (i.e., a veil). *Aletheuein* is the antonym of *lanthano* (to

conceal). *Aletheia*, then, means "an unveiled mystery"—
truth which presents itself, and otherwise inaccessible to
"technical reason." The unveiled mystery of which the
New Testament speaks and with which Christian faith has
to do is the mystery of God unveiled in Jesus Christ. Each
time the word occurs in a substantive sense in the New
Testament, it refers to man's relationship to God, now
revealed or unveiled at God's initiative, in and through the
event of Jesus Christ. Truth is the revelation of God's
power to transform men's fears and guilt and impotence
and humiliation into a sense of bedrock security based on
trust and confidence in God. The truth about God is that
he is pure, unbounded love, and all the consequences that
follow from *this* "state of affairs."

This is "the truth" into which the Holy Spirit is sent to
guide us—and which will make us free from the threat of
meaningless existence (existence as merely discursive).

I have been suggesting to you, in a very sketchy way, that
there are two *dimensions* of truth, corresponding to the
two dimensions of *being*. The one is *the truth about
creation*—and the search for this truth is the proper and
urgent business of the human creature. The method
proper to such study is the method of critical inquiry, the
methods of the liberal arts and the exact sciences. Science,
technology, history, and culture—these are the fruits of
such inquiry, and they are man's responsibility as well as
his proper avenues of effort and achievement. Man's
proper disposition toward all such questions about the creation is curiosity, reality thinking, and the rigorous application of all relevant canons of "verification."

But there is another dimension of truth—*the truth about
the Creator*—and this is rooted and grounded in the in-
effable mystery that surrounds and suffuses our existence.

This truth (*aletheia*) is even more crucial for the *quality* of our existence and the significance of all our learning. The truth of God's grace is not discursive, and it cannot be handled or possessed, either by the wise or the holy. This truth is learned and expressed in worship and devotion— in the life of faith, hope, and love.

This is not a doctrine of "double truth," and I certainly do not imply a hierarchical subordination of the one to the other. These two dimensions of truth coexist—they must be co-related in the life of the Christian college. They must never be posed as alternatives or rivals to each other, nor be subordinated either to the other. The Christian college ought to be a community of persuasion in which truth is sought, in all its "fullness"—but where it is never simply imposed. These two dimensions of truth must not corrupt each other, as they will if either is contemptuous of the other. The aim of the Christian college is to be a community of rigor *and* reverence, of inquiry *and* worship, of competence *and* compassion, truth *and* love. In such a place there would be an "atmosphere" which would prompt men to acknowledge their need for faith and yet would also protect their right to withhold commitment until honestly persuaded.

There is a theological grounding for the distinction I am trying to develop. It is based on the relation, in Christian thought, between the doctrines of creation and redemption. Christian faith begins and ends with the truth of God in Christ. But the revelation of God in Christ is also the true revelation of God the Creator Father. If we know God as Redeemer, then we are truly free to inquire into any and all aspects of his creation, because we thereby know our place in that creation, vis-à-vis the Creator. The freedom to know is rooted in self-knowledge, and self-knowledge is rooted in our knowledge of God's knowledge of us as selves, as subjects of his redemptive love.

Once we understand the distinction between creation and redemption, we can then distinguish between what God is "responsible for" in our existence and what we are responsible for. As Creator Redeemer, he is responsible for our creation, preservation, salvation, and destiny—and this because of our relation to him as *his* creatures. It was "for us men and our salvation" that the Word of God "was made man." This is a truth which bursts on us as an "unveiled Mystery." Yet, as Creator Redeemer, God has also chosen to give his human creatures both the capacity and the responsibility for "tending the creation." Thus, we are responsible for human science and technology, for our culture and art, for our history and politics, as free and responsible creations. This is the plain import of Scripture:

> Thou hast made him a little lower than the angels and hast crowned him with glory and honor; Thou hast put all things under his feet.

Man's vocation, then, is to live by faith in respect of his salvation and by intelligence in respect of his life in the world. So long as we do not prostitute our intelligence by idolizing it, and so long as we do not abuse our faith by domesticating it, the life of faith and the life of inquiry can concur, to the enrichment of both. When men act as if they are responsible for their own creation and salvation, they become superstitious and fanatical. It is the business of a Christian college to prove, in our day and age, that sound learning and high religion belong together—that the best education has a religious perspective at its center and that valid faith actually spurs men to inquiry which is both disciplined and free.

CHAPTER 6

Natural Order
and Transcendent Order

EDITOR'S INTRODUCTION

It seems in some respects an outrageous thing to suggest that we are living now in a "dark age." The technical achievements that mark our time do not, at first glance, appear to be the products of a benighted moment of history. Yet, writing both as physicist and as theologian, William Pollard insists that by our increasing bondage to that limited portion of reality called "nature," we are imprisoned both intellectually and spiritually. We have consented to a shrunken reality. The loss of the transcendent has led, not alone to a distortion of the parameters of the real, but to a distortion of the nature of the scientific enterprise as well. Science does not lead us directly into the heart of reality, as is popularly assumed; rather, it creates highly artificial situations and permits attention only to highly specialized phenomena, while leaving other ranges of experience wholly and deliberately out of account. When, then, we claim omnicompetence for the scientific method and insist that the humanities as well as the sciences conform themselves to it, we darken the age. Our human sensibilities generally, and science particularly, require a new awareness of the supernatural; and since the university has so regularly been the agent of the shrunken world, Pollard believes that it is the special burden of colleges and universities now to encourage the growth of that new awareness.

William G. Pollard is Executive Director of the Oak Ridge Associated Universities.

William G. Pollard
Natural Order
and Transcendent Order

Mᴏʀᴇ ᴛʜᴀɴ ᴀɴʏ ᴏᴛʜᴇʀ ɪɴꜱᴛɪᴛᴜᴛɪᴏɴ ᴏꜰ ꜱᴏᴄɪᴇᴛʏ, ᴛʜᴇ ᴜɴɪ-
versity maintains and nourishes the spirit of the age. If
domination of the oncoming generation by typically scientific styles of thought is to be relieved somewhat, and recovery of the strength and power of the Judeo-Christian
heritage of Western man begun, it is the university which
must do it. My thesis is that modern man has lost a capacity to respond to and to know a whole range of reality
external to himself which Western man in earlier centuries
quite naturally possessed. My purpose is to challenge the
university to seek actively recovery of this lost capacity.

Every age is the victim of its own style of thought. One
does not generally see this about his own age, but in the
retrospect of history, when the style of thought has
changed radically, one can see it about past ages. In re-
counting the history of the rise of science, it is common to
express amazement at the blindness of medieval scholastic
thought. Many questions which the Schoolmen attempted
to answer by appeals to authority could easily have been

Abridged from "The Recovery of Theological Perspective in a Scientific
Age," by William G. Pollard, in *Religion and the University*, published
by the University of Toronto Press for York University, 1964. Reprinted
by permission of York University, University of Toronto Press, and the
author.

settled empirically. It is astounding to us that it never seemed to occur to anyone then simply to observe how things actually were, or to make simple experimental tests of their conclusions. In retrospect we can see clearly, as they could not, how inescapably imprisoned they were in their particular system and style of thought.

What are the characteristics of our contemporary style of thought? What is the particular secret imaginative background which colors our efforts to experience and to know reality? First, the contemporary style consistently avoids all reference to reality transcendent to space and time. Science is by definition the study of nature. By nature we mean the sum total of objects and events in three-dimensional space and time. It is the mission of science to go as far as it can in understanding all objects and events in space and time in terms of other objects and events in space and time. Any mode of understanding in which any aspect of nature depends on something transcendent to nature is not scientific understanding. Science as such does not reject such modes of understanding; it simply ignores them. It cannot do anything else and still be science. This produces a style of thought in which the transcendent and the supernatural simply never appear.

An age such as ours which has lost a genuine capacity for knowing and responding to some great segment of reality is actually, without knowing it, in a dark age. There is, of course, so much sparkle and achievement in present-day science that it seems incredible to speak of the twentieth century as a dark age. Yet I am convinced that several centuries from now in the restrospect of history it is bound to be recognized as such, in spite of all its admitted accomplishments in the area of the natural. We really have lost a genuine capacity which the rest of mankind has possessed and actively exercised, and we have become a people trapped and in bondage within the prison of space, time, and matter. The achievements which make this the golden age of science have led to this imprisonment and made it at the same time a dark age.

As I see it, the primary need is to recover a sense of the existence of a realm of supernature as a genuine part of external reality which is everywhere and always in immediate contact with the realm of nature. In the contemporary dark age this is exceedingly difficult to do. So much that used to be regarded as supernature has vanished by incorporation into nature that many persons suppose that science has positively established the nonexistence of any supernatural realm whatever. But this is clearly not the case. When I am working or thinking as a physicist, I am automatically confined to objects or phenomena in three-dimensional space and time. Whatever reality transcendent to space and time there may be, I would not even know where to begin to observe or explore it by the methods of physics. The whole theoretical structure of modern physics is spatiotemporal. Every discovery of some new particle or antiparticle or of some new phenomenon is a discovery of some aspect of nature previously unknown. Every advance in physics is ultimately a way of comprehending patterns of objects and events in space and time in some larger or more general perspective. Science is by definition the study of nature. It possesses no means whatever of deciding either for or against any aspect of external reality which transcends the realm of nature. If the realm of supernature exists at all, it must be known and experienced in ways which lie wholly outside the scope of science.

An analogy which I have found most helpful for recovering a sense of the reality of supernature as well as its relationship to nature is provided by a small book of the last century by an English mathematician, Edwin Abbott, with the title *Flatland*. It is a story about a two-dimensional universe of infinite extent. Throughout the story three-dimensional observers from spaceland are able to see, as the flatlanders cannot, how the whole of flatland is immersed in space. For the flatlanders the natural order is the sum total of objects and events in their two-dimensional domain. Everything else is for them supernatural. A sphere which visits flatland can enter or leave it at will at any point in it simply by moving perpendicular to the plane which constitutes the flatland universe. When he does, his "natural" component from the flatlander vantage point is the circle of his intersection with this plane. The rest of the sphere is his supernatural component.

The significance of *Flatland* lies in its capacity to awaken in a modern reader the thought that his own three-dimensional universe might be immersed in a larger, though invisible, reality in a way analogous to that in which flatland is immersed in space. It is effective in causing its readers to question the prevailing assumption that the visible domain of three-dimensional space constitutes the totality of all real existence external to man. Moreover, it provides a far more suitable framework on which to hang the universal human experiences of supernatural reality than does the prescientific picture of a supernatural realm up in the sky populated by nonmaterial stars, planets, sun, and moon. Heaven is no longer either "up there" or "out there," as Bishop Robinson puts it, but perpendicular to and in immediate contact with every point of space. Such a framework is directly applicable to the sense of the immediacy and all-pervasiveness of the divine presence which is so powerfully expressed in Psalm 139. Indeed, this sense of all natural things and places being aglow, as it were, with supernatural overtones is much more prominent in Biblical thought than is the "three-story" cosmology with God and heaven "up there" which Israel simply shared with the rest of the ancient world.

The use of *Flatland* in this way is of course only an analogy and doubtless cannot be pushed too far. An even more direct and convincing way, perhaps, to modern man's recovery of a sense of the reality of that which transcends the natural order is provided by Rudolf Otto's classic, *The Idea of the Holy*. This book surveys the whole of mankind's experience of the holy in many different cultures and settings. It is a scholarly piece of work carried out in a spirit and an approach which are entirely agreeable to the modern scientific style of thought. Yet the sheer universality and integrity of what Otto calls *numinous* experience becomes convincing evidence that one is here dealing with an elemental human capacity for experiencing and knowing reality beyond oneself. The object of the numinous experience, which Otto effectively calls the *mysterium tremendum,* seems to be as definite a part of external reality as rocks and trees and atoms. Underneath all the errors and superstitions which have grown up around this category of experience, there is something *real* which only an age that dogmatically rejects all supernatural reality could fail to grasp.

At this point I wish to turn to a related question, namely, the interaction of the supernatural with the natural. More specifically, I wish to consider the reality of God's action in a universe governed by scientific laws and the related question of divine providence in its Biblical sense. Here we have to do with the dominant conviction of modern thought that the explanation for everything which happens in space and time is to be found within space and time. In its extreme form this conviction expresses itself in mechanistic determinism. But even those who would explicitly reject a thoroughgoing mechanical determination of events are still likely to feel that the only real causes are natural causes, and that whatever explanation there may be for events in nature must be sought within nature. In contrast, the Biblical view sees the whole natural order, the world and its history, as continuously responsive to the will and purpose of its Creator, so that the explanation for the course of history must be sought in such categories as grace, judgment, redemption, providence.

The key to a coalescence of the scientific view and the Biblical view lies in achieving a proper perspective on the character of the general laws of nature and the part they play in the shaping of events. Most people, I am convinced, have an erroneous view of the way in which the scientific laws operate. It is a view derived mainly from the character and expectations of nineteenth-century science and modeled on the sure and accurately predictable motions of the planets and their satellites. It conceives of the laws of nature as rigorously determining the course which any system in the universe must follow in each of its individual components. Actually, however, throughout the whole range of the sciences, from physics through biology to psychology and sociology, the laws of nature as they are now known and formulated are almost entirely statistical in character. There are generally several alternative modes of response in the same situation, and the laws of science govern the probabilities of each of them. A familiar example is life insurance in which life expectancies or the probability of death by any given age can be accurately predicted, but the time of death in individual cases cannot.

Because of this statistical character of scientific law, the best that can be done through science is to predict the most probable course of events. Divine providence in its Biblical sense, however, manifests itself chiefly in those crucial turning points at which history takes a most improbable turn. The boundary between the natural and the supernatural determinants of history is formed by chance and accident. So long as things go rather much as expected, everything seems quite natural and dependable. But the really great and decisive moments in which the major achievements of life and history are made are just those which were least expected and most surprising in their occurrence. It is precisely in such events that God's action manifests itself and we are made aware of a divine purpose mysteriously working itself out in history. Such events do not violate natural laws. They are simply so improbable or so accidental as to be essentially indeterminate and unpredictable in terms of the laws of nature.

A comment of the distinguished physicist, J. Robert Oppenheimer, in his Reith lectures is relevant here: "We think . . . of general laws and broad ideas as made up of the instances which illustrate them, and from an observation of which we may have learned them. Yet this is not the whole. The individual event, the act, goes far beyond the general law. It is a sort of intersection of many generalities, harmonizing them in one instance as they cannot be harmonized in general." [1]

We often fail to appreciate how highly artificial are the situations in science in which the regularities of nature are revealed. Each experiment in which some law of nature is verified represents great ingenuity and highly developed technical skill on the part of the scientist performing it. It must exclude a variety of extraneous influences which are always present in the natural, nonlaboratory situation. It rigorously restricts what may happen to precisely that controlled sequence of events in which the particular law, and no other, is operative. In the individual event or act in history, however, many separate trains of causal sequences intersect, as Oppenheimer says. Complex apparatus would be required in the laboratory to isolate each such sequence from the others so as to see what general laws were operative in that aspect of the total event. The laws are all there and operative in the complex fabric of the total situation. But in the event itself, they are all gathered at a particular moment and harmonized by that gathering in the achievement of the end which in retrospect the event is seen to have brought about. It is only in that harmony that the total reality of both the natural and the supernatural domains becomes evident. The supernatural dimension remains invisible and empirically inaccessible. But if it were not there as an integral determinant of the total event, there would be no harmony.

My purpose in this lecture has been to attempt to bring out the way in which the problem of theology and science in our time is basically a problem of the style of thought characteristic of our age. We are to a greater or lesser extent victims of that secret imaginative framework of thought which our culture has instilled in us from infancy and which colors our whole outlook. Within the bondage of that framework, theology—with its concentration on the structure of supernatural reality, its categories of grace, sin, and providence, its insistence on the actuality and key importance of supernatural events in history, such as the incarnation, resurrection, and ascension—seems unreal, alien to the spirit of the age, and without any valid reference in external reality. Yet if modern man only finds the way to recover his lost capacity of response to reality transcendent to space, time, and matter, all this could be changed. It is possible then to imagine a liberated and less restrictive mode of thought in which both theology and science have full range and scope—the one illuminating the character of supernature and the other the character of nature.

My venture into Christian theology is relatively recent, being confined exclusively to the past dozen years of my life. Prior to that, I was completely immersed in the scientific community and my outlook on any question completely dominated by the scientific habit of mind. In the early part of this venture theology was of course for me a whole new thought world. My reaction then to this new world was centered chiefly around the resolution of what seemed at first to be conflicts between science and theology. The more I have wrestled with these supposed conflicts, however, the more I have become aware of that secret, imaginative framework of thought which was coloring the way in which I dealt with every question. The whole experience has been one of a growing sense of liberation from a too-restrictive way of looking at things. It is something comparable to the exhilarating sense of release which early men of the Renaissance experienced. I covet this same kind of liberation for university students today, particularly because it is primarily the business of the university to maintain and transmit the contemporary mode and style of thought and so to maintain the imprisonment of our time. It saddens me to see a new generation being victimized by this all-pervasive spirit of this epoch.

What is important is to share our Judeo-Christian heritage with students in a way which makes it clear that it is concerned with external reality just as much as is science.

Too often it seems to the students to be associated with an outmoded and discredited world view. In that case no matter how moving and powerful its literary treasures may be, it does not seem to the students to represent genuine knowledge. Only as it is seen to provide genuine insight into the character of supernatural reality does it become exciting and relevant to modern man. This achievement is difficult in the contemporary world, but it only makes the task all the more challenging. There is so much pressure for conformity to accepted canons of inquiry in every academic community, so great a tendency to pass on to the next generation the same style and system of thought in which the present generation is already trapped, that few institutions are likely to rise to this challenge. If, as I believe, we are in a dark age and a renaissance of recovery of lost capacities of response to reality is now under way, though largely hidden, the university which takes the leadership in participating in this renaissance will in time stand out as a great center of renewal. That is an exciting prospect.

CHAPTER 7

Limited Cognition
and Ultimate Cognition

EDITOR'S INTRODUCTION

A formidable educational wall of separation has arisen in the minds of those who have been negatively impressed by the formal relationships between churches and colleges they have observed and who therefore judge such relationships as chiefly repressive and unwise. Before a college impatiently severs these ties to set sail upon what it imagines to be the balmy seas of freedom and of governmental aid, it would do well to consider the mutual benefits in the relationship which Robert Friedrichs sets forth. Both the college and the church gain from a positive relationship, he holds. Not only are faculty members and students in such a college holders of a special freedom to pursue cognitive ultimacy and its valuational base; they are also free to offer their own valuational base for critical examination. Further, they are not required to be detached specialists but can be free and responsible as whole persons to witness to other whole persons. The college, in turn, by exercising its academic calling serves the church by preventing her from "compromising herself with easy answers to the complexity of her calling." It helps the church resist the temptation to nurture outmoded symbols or to "harbor semantic hypocrisy." Finally, in acknowledging the limits of rationality in its own operation, the college simultaneously reminds the church of the limits of exhortation and helps it remain aware that it is by grace that men are saved.

Robert W. Friedrichs is Professor of Sociology in Drew University.

Robert W. Friedrichs
Limited Cognition
and Ultimate Cognition

How might church and university reciprocate within the format of the church college while each maintains its separate integrity?

The church has again and again demonstrated its unwillingness to confront man except in terms of his wholeness and his link with that which is ultimate. And these are the very dimensions of his existence which public and private education in general have been unwilling or unable to engage. Here lies the vocation of the church college. Secularity by its very definition remains stranded with the division and specialization of function, with a rootless relativity, with man defined as means, with change itself as focal value. The church college has the freedom to risk responsibility in depth.

More particularly, it possesses the freedom to encourage its faculties—to select them if need be—to push the student beyond the professional-dictated confines of his discipline so that the student approaches ultimacy in its cognitive forms: in an examination of the discipline's epistemological, and thus ontological, presuppositions; in the following of a

Abridged from "The Church and College in Reciprocal Service," by Robert W. Friedrichs, *motive*, April, 1966. Reprinted by permission of *motive*, copyright 1966.

given proposition to its ultimate implication; in perceiving
the potential relatedness of all the separate wares hawked
in the academic marketplace. Public and private secular
schools are not so privileged. They need share no faith
in the purposiveness and relatedness of the totality of existence. Their charge is from the piecemeal god of secularity.
Their hands are tied and their agents subtly punished
when they step beyond the curricular divisions and segmented roles of the secular city. Faculties of church-related
universities are charged instead to speak and act and write
beyond the limits of academic respectability, to be fools,
academic fools, for the Christ that confronts them—or indeed for the absent Christ, to witness to his loss. They are
and must remain free to trace the trail that ultimately
wends throughout the world of the cognitive.

But they should do more. They are not allowed, as their
secular cohorts may be, to confess that education is *but*
cognition. They may not rest upon the laurels of their
intellectual virtuosity; they are asked to be honest as well.
And honesty calls for the acknowledgment that cognitive
models or predispositions—their own as well as those of
others—rest upon preference, upon choice, upon implicit
if not explicit valuation. Their fortunate fellows in secular
institutions may expect—indeed are encouraged—to close
shop once the cognitive wares have been placed on display.
The church-related scholar must draw himself within the
circle, must accept engagement within class as well as
without, must acknowledge and act upon the existential
roots of his own intellectual structures. He must, in other
words, witness to his own confrontation with ultimacy so
that the cognitive wares he sells may be confronted in their
entirety. For the Christian faith stands not upon formula;
it risks its footing quite explicitly in faith. Though the

secular academician is equally unable to take his stand upon cognition alone, he has no obligation to confess the fact to his students or to his colleagues. His secular context encourages him to perceive his action as segmented into roles, and the role of cognition and the role of the man of faith, like state and church, are to be insulated one from another.

The focal service the church *might* provide the university, then, is a dedication to ultimates in the cognitive sphere and the engagement of those ultimates honestly and openly with the existential self. Both follow from a confrontation with the church's faith in the purposive unity of God's acts of creation. Following from these, as the second great commandment grows out of the first, should be that special sensitivity to one's fellow creatures which causes them to be perceived as ends rather than as means. Though it is an ethic that has come to be shared with many who speak in the secular mode, it is all too easily lost sight of as the university accepts the bed and board of the state and is transformed by sheer numbers into the secular city itself.

The church institution is in a position to say that the clean lines of efficiency, however admirable they may be, are not next to godliness. Secular schools may wish to avoid the electronization of the educational process. But viewing it only as cognitive communication and but sentimentally attached to man as person, they are rapidly capitulating to its bureaucratization and routinization. The church college does so at the peril of denying itself. One can communicate with machines; machines can communicate with each other: but machines cannot *witness to* one another. Thus the church-related institution is commanded to witness to the integrity of the I-Thou in the processes of education as well as in its content, to insure that the professor risks something of himself through the dialectical impact of teacher upon student and student upon teacher.

Finally, the church is in a position to guarantee the integrity of academia's prophetic mode against subtle temptations toward professional disengagement and the less subtle incursions of the morality of the state. Its academic freedom is not freedom *from,* but freedom *to;* not protection *against,* but responsibility *for.* Obligation upon its campuses does not end with the code of ethics of one's discipline, with the legislation of the AAUP, or with the flags of one's state and nation. It can end only at the foot of the cross.

But what of the reciprocal contribution of the university? Is the creature of the church still but recipient? Certainly its original function as a preparatory school for the clergy has long since withered. And few Protestant colleges can still claim that the majority within their student bodies may be expected to become lay leaders within their denomination. The campus may provide facilities for conferences for their clergy and/or selected laymen, but the very fact that such meetings are scheduled so that they will not interfere with the academic calendar witnesses to their peripheral nature. What, then, can be left?

In its dedication to truth wherever it may lead, the academic community may act to prevent the church from compromising herself with easy answers to the complexity of her calling. It does so through the painstaking delineation of the empirical from the existential, of nature from history, of philosophy from theology. It serves thus as a guarantor of the integrity of the creation, assisting the church thereby to speak of and witness to its Author and his ever-present power to create anew.

The contemporary "death of God" theology—nourished not by accident at our church-related universities—illustrates a second outgrowth of this truth commitment. For what is pointed to metaphorically is the university's insistence that it must assist the church to tag and bury every temptation upon the latter's part to harbor semantic hypocrisy. Intellectual honesty—to God and to his creation—demands the cleansing of our symbolic life, the media by which I seeks to communicate with Thou, just as existential honesty demands the cleansing of the self. God's mighty act of creation goes on, oblivious of our hope to package it in neat categories once and for all. The university's sensitivity to the historicity of our linguistic models stands as a continual reminder that God not only was and is, but is yet to be.

Thus the academic community that is in responsible relationship with the church will find itself exorcizing those images in our common vocabulary whose contemporary coloration would deny our Lord by cataloging him among the artifacts of the museum of man. Our Lord liveth. The university reminds us that our symbol life does as well. It not only would deny us the psychic security of linguistic hysteria, but it seeks to sensitize us to those symbols which appear at the cutting edge of each new generation's confrontation with its uniqueness. If God is to live, then the metaphors by which we approach him must equally live. This fact the university can assist us in confronting.

Of perhaps less significance, yet relevant, might be the university's intimate awareness of the limits of its own prime strength: its rationality. It is important that the Protestant church, relying so heavily upon the preaching of the Word—upon exhortation—be reminded of the irrational roots of rationality. This the university may be in a privileged position to do, for in pushing back the curtain of cognition as far as it will go, it has had to confront in depth the factuality of the unconscious, the resistances of cultural patterns and social structures, the ultimate privacy of the intrasubjective, and the screen by which language filters reality. All these may help the church to remain aware that it is by God's grace and not her exhortation that we shall be saved.

Finally, it is well to remind ourselves that, in an age in which the church seeks reunion and the world at large its first slender strands of unity, "university" is literally a place in which all are turned (*versum*) toward one (*unus*). If ecumenicity is indeed an appropriate characterization of the openness and intimacy we seek from one another, there are perhaps no better exercise grounds—perhaps no better models—than those evolved in the name of the university.

Unfortunately, the church and the university *are* largely but institutions—caught up as institutional life is today in the segmented flux of the secular city. No perceptive sociologist is in a position to deny the general descriptive and predictive logic of Harvey Cox's conclusion that the "organized church" no longer has a distinctive role vis-à-vis the university. Church colleges may be expected to continue to degenerate into functional appendages of that city, distinguished only as havens for the socially advantaged who seek the succor of a familiar institutional identification. Yet no Biblically informed man can deny, either, that God somehow calls forth a saving remnant to witness to the possibilities of his creation.

CHAPTER 8

Academic Teaching and Human Experience

EDITOR'S INTRODUCTION

Immediately below the surface of the "subject matter" that professors and their students pull and stretch and count the fibers of, throb the ultimate questions of life and death and destiny, the human experience of transitoriness and fragility and uniqueness. Yet students are asked to work at the surface of academic matters as though there were no pulsing depths beneath them. They are trained to become "intellectual technologists," professionals who deal "objectively" with "facts." If man—let alone God—is to return to the campus, however, argues Mr. Novak, the questions and experiences that are labeled "subjective," that call forth conviction and demand commitment, must become matters for passionate academic debate. Commitment and learning belong together.

Michael Novak is Associate Professor of Religious Studies and Chairman of the Humanities Seminar, State University of New York, College at Old Westbury.

Michael Novak

Academic Teaching
and Human Experience

Although the colleges pride themselves on the awakening of young minds, on the asking of the Big Questions of life (who and what is man, whence has he come, where is he going, what is love, what is passion, what is reason, is there a God?), it is soon clear to college students that the Big Questions don't count—either in academic standing, or in later life, or in research grants.

In the first place, the standing assumption is that ultimate questions are in principle unanswerable, and hence not worth asking seriously. This assumption may not discourage freshmen, but over a four-year period it is pretty well driven home. In the second place, nobody is much interested in students' answers to such questions, or deems them worth putting in competition with anybody else's. Even among the professors it is assumed that ultimate questions are nonintellectual, personal, and if matters of supreme importance and self-commitment, nevertheless not matters for passionate academic dispute. The university, on principle, concentrates on statistics, historical facts, historical intellectual positions, logic modeled on the discourse

Abridged from "God in the Colleges," by Michael Novak, *Harper's Magazine*, October, 1961. Copyright © 1961 by Michael Novak. Reprinted by permission of Curtis Brown, Ltd.

of the physical sciences, and ample documentation. Even the literature courses, under the impact of the New Criticism, have the students noting the occurrences of words, running down allusions, and abstracting from the conditions of history. The Anglo-American university has committed itself to all that is "objective," countable, precise, publicly verifiable. Though this commitment suits the middle-class temper capitally, it stifles religion almost to death.

Not only religion is stifled. More fundamentally, it is possible—it is even common—for a student to go to class after class of sociology, economics, psychology, literature, philosophy, and the rest, and hardly become aware that he is dealing with issues of life and death, of love and solitude, of inner growth and pain. He may never fully grasp the fact that education is not so much information and technique as self-confrontation and change in his own conscious life. He may sit through lectures and write examinations—and the professors may *let* him do merely that—collecting verbal "answers," without really thinking through and deciding about any new aspect of his own life in any course. The dilemma of education has always been to combine merely mental skills with personal experiencing and growth. The educational currents in American colleges tend to oscillate from one pole to the other, and at present the attention in college to the formal and the public easily leaves the inner life of the student untouched.

Middle-class Christianity—the bourgeois Christianity which Nietzsche, Kierkegaard, Peguy, Bloy, and others so hated—was always prudent, small-visioned, secure. It dared little, with its gaudy-colored plaster statues or its devices to protect the little world of the entrepreneur. In the person of many university professors, middle-class secular humanism is not much more daring. It thinks of itself as humble in its agnosticism and eschews the "mystic flights" of metaphysicians, theologians, and dreamers; it is cautious and remote in dealing with heightened and passionate experiences that are the stuff of much great literature and philosophy. It limits itself to this world and its concerns, concerns which fortunately turn out to be largely subject to precise formulation, and hence have a limited but comforting certainty. (It has a particularly comfortable ambience if it works within the physical sciences, or mathematics, or the statistics of sociology and economics.)   If we cannot control the great uncertain questions in the universe, nevertheless we can make a universe of little certainties we can control.

The agnosticism—atheism would be too strong a word— of the classroom is not militant.   It is only, in principle, unconcerned.   It is bourgeois Christianity all over again, to so great an extent that, in college, in spite of differences in belief, the behavior of agnostic and of religious man is pretty much the same.

The agnosticism of the classroom does not have to be militant.   Once upon a time it was fighting for its life; now it is an accepted part of the college scene, in fact the predominating part.   The old battles between positive science and religion which delighted, or angered, our grandfathers—about chance and design, monkeys and Adam—seldom resound now in academic halls.   The distinction between empirical and theological activity seems pretty well recognized—each side preserves a certain calm and only occasionally do tempers flare.   Perhaps psychologists more than others are given to writing off religion as illusion; anthropologists, in turn, are habituated to data on revelations and recurrent religious themes, and correspondingly casual about the traditions of Judaism and Christianity. One school of analysis in philosophy, of which Russell and Ayer among others are examples, believes that nothing that cannot be reduced to sense experience can have meaning, and most religious questions of course lie outside this restricted zone. Some partisans of another movement, linguistic analysis, following the later Wittgenstein, do not require the discourse of faith and theology to conform to other kinds of discourse, but study it in its own right; but religion does not lie in words.

Professional disciplines aside, a bland tolerance seems to be everybody's ideal. Say nothing that will offend. Say nothing that involves personal commitment. Stay close to the public facts. "You've got to teach these youngsters to forget the *shoulds* and *musts* they came here with," one new teaching fellow was recently admonished by his program director. "The students have to learn to be objective." And of course such a critique is excellent, since some *shoulds* and *musts* are what a man dies for. But there seems to be correspondingly little concern about which ones he will acquire and keep.

Professor Raphael Demos, of Harvard, was once quoted as saying, with perhaps his touch of irony, "*Veritas* means we are committed to nothing." It may be that the American consensus has forced a "commitment to nothing" upon our universities; we are a pluralist people, and it seems very difficult to discover a way to teach about those differences on ultimate questions that make us so. The colleges make a "commitment to noncommitment," have a "faith in non-faith." They demand perpetual reexamination and have nowhere to rest.

Thus the new middle-class tolerance of the colleges neither destroys—nor transforms—the religion of the incoming freshmen. Of one hundred students who marked themselves "atheistic or agnostic" on the poll of the Harvard *Crimson* in 1959, only ten felt "obliged . . . to enlighten others to abandon their faith." The new tolerance merely establishes, officially and in principle, that personal conviction be separated from teaching and learning. If a student wishes to commit himself to answers to ultimate questions (by commitment to some personal synthesis, or to traditional religion or ethics, or anything), he may do so—is even encouraged to do so—but not publicly, nor officially, not in his daily work. He will do well to keep his answers to himself. In term papers and on tests they will not be welcome; there he is obliged to prove rather that he knows facts and correlations, and can run, seeking, as well as anyone else. No one in *official* university life seems to care about his convictions.

There is good reason for the university's position. One of its tasks is to turn out professional men. Think of the difficulty there would be in correcting exams and term papers if each student were engaged in a highly personal way in working out a position important to himself. What if the student found that something of importance to him was of minor importance to the course—or outside its confines? The dilemma of professionalism versus full human experience is a pressing one, and cannot be solved by making light of it.

Although it is not clear what constitutes religious "strength," it is clear that if the student's faith goes through a personal trial-by-fire, that is his affair. There are few courses in critical theology, few in modern critical Biblical theory, few in the theory and practice of organized religion, to help him explicitly and formally to mature his theological intelligence. In the view of some religious men, this is a good thing; religion, after all, is not something that can be formally taught. It is a living commitment to be enkindled from person to person, a life to be lived rather than lessons to be learned. Besides, formal theological studies imply a living content of religious experience, but it is precisely this living content which in our day most men no longer possess. If religion is to enter the university, it must enter first at the most elementary level: in experience, in awareness, in slow and gradual exploration. The traditional words are not relevant to the present religious development of most men. Our times are sub-, not only post-, religious. The institutionalized forms of religion did not originate in modern life, and modern science and technology have grown up outside them; the two worlds of religion and modernity are strangers to each other. Were there to be merely formal courses in theology at the university, genuine religious life would fare hardly better than at present. As the New Criticism is to art, so is critical theology to religious awareness. Theology, like the New Criticism, has a role to play, but it is neither necessary nor sufficient for religious life.

If we admit that theologians would also contribute to the professionalism and formalism already thriving in the modern university, who might do better? The answer, I suggest, must be that the greatest contribution to the religious life of the university could come from teachers and scholars—formally religious or not—who could lead the student to the profound human experiences lying below the surface of the academic curriculum.

These experiences are often "prereligious"; they are barely starting points for full religious life. But they are the only foundation on which anything living can be built. I mean man's experience of his fragility, of his transitoriness, of his tininess; his consciousness of his uniqueness on the earth, of his endless and restless questioning; his personal choices whose motives and consequences he cannot fully know; his vast ability to be proud and to fail, to be isolated and to love, to be—and yet not to be—the master of his own destiny.

These experiences, and others like them, underlie the statistics of economics and of sociology, the laws and hypotheses of psychology, philosophy, and other disciplines; they are at the source of great poems and novels and histories now often taught as if they were technical puzzles.

Large and unsettling personal questions arise from these experiences. And it is by their answers, explicit or implicit, that men finally differ from one another: how they react to achievement, to pride, to love, to suffering, to feelings of life and energy, to death. Implicit in the actions of every man is his own particular bias and approach to economics, to social and political affairs, to all matters with which he deals. What are the biases and beliefs that make a student unique and color all his judgments even in his professional concerns? Instead of concentrating on this question, and hence helping the student toward self-discovery, the university takes the easier path: it tries to maintain an area of "objectivity" and "fact." But the truly crucial element in human knowing (I repeat: even in professional knowing) lies in the recesses of personal judgment. Our critical sciences, unlike our creative arts, have favored the "objective" over the "subjective." Our universities favor the one pole over the necessary two: notional-verbal competence, over the self-knowledge and self-commitment that also affect professional careers and make up personal life.

Meanwhile, the student on the secular campus works out his religion for himself. Often his previous religious background will have been uncritical, informal, and unsophisticated; he may be the first member of his family pursuing a university education. His grasp of religious concepts like faith, hope, love, may well be far less precise and intellectually defensible than it ought to be; his university career will offer him very little formal help in clarifying and criticizing them. It is possible that college life may be for him, then, a period of searing but private examination. For a time at least he may stop going to church or synagogue and believe himself atheist or agnostic. But the chances are—in most schools and among most students—no such honest and fruitful personal critiques will occur, at least of any lasting depth. Where they do seem to occur, experienced religious men are pleased. "It's a more thoughtful kind of religion" seems to be the consensus of chaplains near Harvard. "It's better than merely going to church out of habit. They may be missing church services and undergoing changes now; but they'll be back when they return to their local communities and all the better for it."

But will they be? The fact seems to be that even among the more searching students, religion follows the pattern of their other personal convictions. The pattern of conformity they are taught in college, by which they systematically separate their inner convictions from the "objective" work of the classroom, will simply be continued in their business affairs, legal practice, or work of whatever kind in later life. A civilization pervaded by the laws and spirit of technology—on which profit and life itself are based—is a civilization prone to expediency and nonmoral, nonpersonal considerations. The vice of academicians is to become intellectual technologists; this vice prevails. The consequent bourgeois life of the American university becomes with hardly a hitch the middle-class life of the organiza-

tion man and the suburbanite. The pretense of noncon-
formity and intellectual liberty on campus is seldom tested
by real and fundamental disagreement; for such disagreement is usually "subjective" and not amenable to the kind
of debate the university tacitly approves. "Liberals" and
"conservatives" in politics, for example, seldom touch the
basic issues separating them; they both try to argue in
terms of "facts"; but why they are committed, each in his
separate way, to different ideals, and what precisely these
ideals are and whence they are derived—this kind of discussion does not suit the pragmatic and "objective" temper
of present intellectual life. It is too intangible, dialectical,
personal, however lethal in its effect upon action.

One might have hoped that the religiously committed
private schools in America might have made by now some
major contribution to American intellectual life. In part,
they have been too concerned with putting up buildings,
with more or less ghettolike defensiveness, and with hesi-
tating between secular standards and their own long-ago
tradition. In part, general American intellectual life rules
out of professional discussion the very commitment which
the religious schools primarily exist to foster. In any case,
the potential strength of the religious school now goes
almost for nought.

One might have hoped that religious men within the
secular colleges might by their understanding and their
leadership have restored to American universities a chance
for a living and critical experience of religion. For decades
there have been too few men at once intellectual and religious and wise on the campuses. Vast empty spaces seem
to surround the Niebuhrs and the Tillichs. The churches
are filled with worshipers, but intelligence has fled from
the ranks of religion. Who or what can bring it back?

What, then, is the place of God in our colleges? The basic human experiences that remind man that he is not a machine, and not merely a temporary cog in a technological civilization, are not fostered within the university. God is as irrelevant in the universities as in business organizations, but so are love, death, personal destiny. Religion can thrive only in a personal universe; religious faith, hope, and love are personal responses to a personal God. But how can the immense question of a personal God even be posed and made relevant when fundamental questions about the meaning and limits of personal experience are evaded?

"God is dead. . . . What are these churches if they are not the tombs and sepulchers of God?" Nietzsche asked. But much of Western humanism is dead too. Men do not wander under the silent stars, listen to the wind, learn to know themselves, question. "Where am I going? Why am I here?" They leave aside the mysteries of contingency and transitoriness for the certainties of research, production, consumption. So that it is nearly possible to say: "Man is dead. . . . What are these buildings, these tunnels, these roads, if they are not the tombs and sepulchers of man?"

God, if there is a God, is not dead. He will come back to the colleges when man comes back.

CHAPTER 9

Academic Excellence and Moral Value

EDITOR'S INTRODUCTION

The contemporary notion of what constitutes the best in education is too deficient in its failure to find a place for moral value at its very center to deserve a longer life as a slogan for higher education. The idea of excellence as the triumphant fulfillment of intellectual talent simply fails to do justice to the depth of the academic disciplines, to the critical challenges of our times, or to the full nature of the student being educated. Commitment to the raising of issues that do justice to these things, however, is fully consonant with the academic enterprise, Editor Jellema maintains. The moral dimension so penetrates and surrounds academic learning that it awaits each advance of research, it is discovered at the profoundest levels of analysis, it accompanies each technological development, it presses for meaning in every discipline. The moral dimension moreover, is what much of contemporary student unrest is about. Students are troubled by the moral magnitude of the questions confronting them and the seeming irrelevance of their curricula. What education cannot forget, finally, is the development of the man who is the user of knowledge. The enlargement of his moral concern is an educational task that ought to proceed in full harmony with the expansion of his intellectual abilities.

William W. Jellema is Executive Associate and Research Director in the Association of American Colleges.

William W. Jellema

Academic Excellence
and Moral Value

THE TROUBLE WITH EXCELLENCE, LOUIS T. BENEZET NOTED,[1] is its use as a "heaven-sent term to explain in one breath the reason for a sharp tuition hike" and its employment as a rationalization for a big build-up in the football program. He objected to the class overtones in the general interpretations of excellence, and to limiting the definition of excellence to a demand for stronger conventional preparation and more diligent study by the students. "Excellence," he said, "is more than academic excellence." With all of this, and more, I am in agreement.

My own disenchantment with excellence goes farther than Mr. Benezet's. What particularly dismays me about the continuance of excellence as a slogan for higher education in our age is the poverty of its nonmoral definition, the virtual absence of concern for moral values. Excellence may have nothing to do with the good life.

Perhaps it is only another example of American exuberance and overambition compounded by a Madison Avenue use of superlatives; perhaps it is merely ludicrous. But is there not something, too, of the tragic flaw in a society that having failed to achieve the good, now pursues the excellent? Having lost sight of the positive which we never quite attained, and with complete and cavalier disregard of the comparative, we now declare ourselves passionately devoted to the superlative.

Our concept of excellence, as John Conway noted, is the triumphant fulfillment of talent. The talent most admired may be athletic, financial, literary, artistic, scholarly—at bottom these are not philosophically different. If a practitioner has been successful in the development of his talent, he has achieved excellence. The educated man is no longer expected to choose the best. Instead, he expects recognition that what he chooses is in fact best and that what he does best is excellent. Adolf Hitler brushed aside any worries whether the propagandistic reason for starting war was plausible or not. "The victor," William L. Shirer quotes him as saying, "will not be asked afterward whether he told the truth or not. In starting and waging a war, it is not right that matters, but victory." [2] Measured by contemporary standards of excellence, Hitler would be found a failure, but not evil.

The concept of excellence as the triumphant fulfillment of talent divorced from moral consideration was classically illustrated by an incident on what was then the Jack Parr show on television. Parr's guest one evening was Burt Lancaster, who had just finished making the picture *The Bird Man of Alcatraz*. This is the story of Robert Stroud, who was committed to Alcatraz for murder and who, during his confinement, began the study that led to the establishment of his reputation as an ornithologist. They had some trouble, Mr. Lancaster related, discovering an appropriate title for this film. He himself, having become enamored of the man and what he was, had suggested, not wholly facetiously, that they entitle it *Robert Stroud, American*. For, he said, and here I paraphrase him, this man exemplified the ideals and the excellence that made America great. Yet, as Mr. Lancaster himself related,

Robert Stroud was repeatedly refused parole because he never at any time showed the slightest remorse for the murder that had put him in Alcatraz.

So thoroughly have we accepted the idea of excellence as the triumphant fulfillment of talent (which in institutions of higher learning is chiefly intellectual talent) that a description of a system that challenges this outlook sounds very peculiar indeed. How strange the remarks that Sydney D. Bailey elicited from one Mr. Han in a conversation which he recorded in 1958.

Out of his Confucianist background, Mr. Han stated his conviction that men are not equal, as two stones may be said to have equal weight.

"Some are of cultivated character and moral excellence," he said, "and these should be accorded due respect."

"Do you then believe in class distinctions?" I asked.

"Yes," replied Mr. Han, "but not those of the kind that I have observed in the West: the class distinctions based upon inherited wealth and property; or the other and worse system based on intellectual attainment. . . .

"These people," he said, astonished at such a state of affairs, "esteem knowledge higher than virtue." In a better-ordered society, "the higher class of person is distinguished by character rather than knowledge. There are some who possess an abundance of information, but they do not thereby acquire nobility of character."

"Would you have wealth confiscated and knowledge suppressed?" I asked.

"Wealth and knowledge both cause pain unless properly used. No man should be entrusted with either until he has discovered the way of wisdom. . . . In the West you honor courage, loyalty, diligence. You regard athletes and actors, bureaucrats and bankers, politicians and professors. . . . As for wisdom, it is rarely honored. You are in such a hurry going to and fro that you do do not even discern wisdom. You mobilize great wealth and great knowledge, and then you merely construct devices of destruction." [3]

Even as late as a generation ago the development of character—a quaint phrase embracing part of what I here seek to promote—was still thought to be an important objective in college education. In fact, some continued to think that even graduate schools had responsibilities in this area. Today few, if any, graduate schools pretend any concern for this kind of education. Most colleges of liberal arts retain some reference to concern for the improvement of character or moral values and issues, but these no longer head the list of objectives. Indeed, to quote Benezet again, "on nine-tenths of the campuses, goals like these, even when written by the faculty themselves, are dismissed as promotional rhetoric or as good things that are bound to happen through exposure to college teaching." [4]

At the Honors Convocation at the University of Michigan in 1967, UN Secretary U Thant said:

Clearly, vocational teaching—how to do a job—and social teaching—how to live in society—are fundamental ingredients of education. There is, I believe, a third essential ingredient which is no less vital for being delicate and highly elusive: I mean moral teaching in the sense of inculcating and keeping alive certain essential values. These values must both correspond to the realities of life in the world today and yet have an inner strength of their own which can withstand the destructive aspects of those realities. [5]

The raising of moral issues within the curriculum of the liberal arts college, it is my purpose to contend, is native to the academic fields of study, pertinent to the times, and essential for the full humanity of the student.

The study of basic principles and basic issues in every area of human learning so often raises a moral issue that it may safely be said that moral issues and moral values pervade the liberal arts curriculum. If, as the philosophers have hoped, the good, the true, and the beautiful are at bottom one, then this pervasion of moral issues in areas that might seem more strictly related to the true and the beautiful is precisely what one would expect to find.

But the moral issue is not only frequently uncovered in the study of basic principles, it is frequently discovered in advanced research. It has been the pursuit of study and research in areas that, on the surface at least, would be considered nonmoral that has brought about the creation or rediscovery of many moral issues in our times. It has been the study and application of science that has presented us with the moral issues of a technological age. Because of research in psychology and biology, Elting I. Morison placed high on his list of desirable new forms of excellence, "a new scheme of morality to deal with the rapidly-developing sense of determinism produced by work in psychology and biology." Sociologists have helped to bring about an increased awareness of a larger society, but this has not gone hand in hand with increased moral perception and moral concern. Indeed, popular sociological conceptions may have weakened moral virility. As Meg Greenfield put it: "Just as psychological interpretations have tended to do away with the doer, so this generous sociological thesis tends to do away with the deed. Guilt, like democracy, is everybody's job." [6]

For a profound conception of morality and for the raising of really significant moral issues, moreover, the profound study of many academic areas is important. Because the moral issue is a native integrating factor in the curriculum, it often ignores the boundaries of the disciplines and cannot be fully seen through a single isolated avenue of investigation.

A second argument that justifies the recognition of moral issues in the curriculum is the high degree of contemporaneity of need present in this area. Moral decision (which cannot be made until men see the moral issue) is needed as never before in history, but man has never before been seemingly so incapable of taking positive action.

I want to avoid appearing to suggest that moral issues and man's need to make moral decisions are something new. After all, the story of Adam and Eve in the Garden of Eden turns upon this theme. Nor are men less moral today than formerly—if by moral is meant endowed with a capacity to be aroused to consideration of right and wrong, good and evil, and of the need to make decisions in this area.

But moral decisions are not pertinent today merely because they have always been present and always will be. There are forces at work that have created special problems and that have made action in the moral sphere more demanding and compelling. At the University of Michigan's Institute on College and University Administration in 1966, Leroy Augenstein entitled an address dealing with the frightening confrontation with decisions in biology as a result of genetic research, "Freedom to Play God." Developments in the biological and behavioral sciences have brought into fresh and sharp perspective the need for an understanding of man's moral responsibility in a seemingly deterministic context. Moreover, the technological age in which we live has added some dimensions to moral issues that were unknown or were less dramatic in the past. Let us look more closely at this last statement.

A technological age has greatly accelerated and exaggerated the problems relating to human obsolescence—problems that have been present in Western civilization since the Industrial Revolution began—without yielding any new answers to these problems. The moral issue is the need to reconsider "efficiency" as the sole standard by which to judge technological change and the need to raise questions about social cause, social justice, or the work orientation of our society.

A technological age has brought about both mass mobility and mass communication and by means of these an awareness of the prevalence of codes of morality at variance with those of the local community. For good or evil, and it seems to have been both, the result has contributed to a breakdown of traditional morality. A man's closest society can no longer be expected to support and transmit a generally-agreed-upon system of values. This throws the man back on his own resources or on those of his immediate family. Where these are insufficient, confusion and anxiety tend to produce a moral paralysis, and the individual finds himself unable to act or acts in unquestioning conformity with a shifting crowd sentiment.

More importantly, a technological age has made the past, together with its morality, seem more irrelevant to this generation than the past did to any preceding generation. The trend, however, was evident before we entered a technological age. A lost sense of history preceded the growth of technology.

A technological age merely accelerated and exaggerated

a philosophical trend that was already definite. But that acceleration has been exponential. There are greater apparent differences in each decade today than there were in each half century or more in days gone by. And with these technological changes, social institutions and outlooks on life change. At the same time, our enthusiastic acceptance of change, our institutionalization of it, our lack of forces opposing it, and our unwillingness to control or guide the direction of change make the future seem equally uncertain and remote.

At an annual conference on higher education, one of the discussion groups directed its attention to the subject "How can students acquire the stability of enduring attitudes, motivation, and knowledge to deal with revolutionary changes ahead?" As judged by the response of the audience and of the panelists themselves, the most devastating question seemed to be that raised by a gentleman in the audience from Denmark who said, in effect, "How do you know that the future will be such that *any* given attitudes and values will be important?" I submit that one way to guarantee that the future will be even more formless and chaotic than the present is to work on the basis of this despair: that there are no enduring and lasting attitudes and values.

As a result of both the past and the future becoming uncertain and remote, both the older and the younger generations, both parents and their children, see the parental model not so much wrong as irrelevant. As a consequence, wrote Kenneth Keniston,

technologies, institutions, ideologies and people—all react by extremes when faced with the fear of obsolescence. Either they may firmly insist that *nothing* has changed and that they are as integrally valid as ever before or—and this is equally disastrous—they become so eager to abandon the outmoded that they abandon essential principles along with the irrelevant. . . . The second alternative seems to me the more prevalent and dangerous. An antiquated outlook is usually simply ignored by the young. But person or institution that abandons its essential principles indirectly communicates that there are no principles which can withstand the test of time, and thus makes the task of the young more difficult.[7]

Finally, recognizing and raising moral issues in the curriculum is justified by the fact that the developed capacity to perceive moral issues and informed ability to make decisions concerning them is essential to man's real humanity. Only at the peril of his humanity can this capacity be voided or avoided. A technological and democratic age has brought Western man closer to the rest of the world and involved him in moral issues of great magnitude. The rise of a democratic nation to a position of world leadership has brought the decision-making responsibility for world war closer to each individual citizen of that nation than to any citizenry before in history, while the "power" of his decision has been greatly increased due to the immense potential of the destructive force. His franchise has given him a responsible hand in world politics; technology has placed the button of destruction within his reach; yet depersonalized man does not seem sufficiently aware of his moral responsibilities. To satisfy our computers, as Paul Reinert once put it, we have permitted a technological age to depersonalize the man who is so directly confronted with moral issues of great magnitude. Even in the moment when he is confronted with a moral issue, we tabulate his moral responses and punch his IBM card. It is this situation which prompted Robert S. Morison to write:

> People in general must not only *know* that what they do affects everyone everywhere and at all times in the future, but they must *care* about it also. Here indeed is a situation that calls for a new sort of excellence—an educational system in the broadest sense that will acquaint people in general with the reality of action at a distance and a concern for that reality.[8]

It is precisely at this point that education as typically conceived and typically executed fails. As Martin Mayer pointed out,[9] because of the "almost mystical belief in education" in this country, for many people the most shocking thing about Hitlerism was that it could occur in *educated* Germany. Shirer's *The Rise and Fall of the Third Reich* is copiously sprinkled with examples of college graduates, Ph.D.'s, professional men, and university professors who were active in their concurrence with the standards of Nazi Germany.

Of them all perhaps the starkest example was supplied by Goebbels, a man who brings to mind the philosopher Berkeley's observation: "He who has not much meditated upon God, the human mind and the *summum bonum*, may possibly make a thriving earth worm, but will most indubitably make a sorry patriot and a sorry statesman." Joseph Goebbels, Ph.D., was the only one of Hitler's henchmen who voluntarily submitted to death with Hitler. So firmly committed were he and his wife to Hitler and his program that prior to taking their own lives they poisoned their six children. Yet his published diaries reveal that Goebbels wrote: "The programme, the spiritual and economic fundamentals, all of that is vague; in my own mind and certainly in the minds of the others." [10] Goebbels is a glaring illustration of the problem: formal education does not often enough succeed in confronting a man with spiritual fundamentals and moral issues, and the result is something less than the fully human. "I thought everyone was born human," Gruner's daughter Angela remarks to Saul Bellow's Arthur Sammler. "It's not a natural gift at all," he answers. "The capacity is natural. The rest is work." And part of that work is the task of formal education.

Perhaps Constantine Zurayk, professor of history at the American University of Beirut and president of the International Association of Universities, put it simply and directly at an international conference commemorating the sesquicentennial of the University of Michigan: "No knowledge will save the world unless infused with moral concern and passionate love." I am inclined to agree.

Part III
NORMS
AND MODELS
OF COMMITMENT

CHAPTER 10

Biblical Realism
as a Norm

EDITOR'S INTRODUCTION

The curriculum of the liberal arts colleges often seems, to many students and other thoughtful observers, removed from and irrelevant to the real lives of real people. Will Herberg agrees with this judgment and argues that the current detachment of the curriculum stems from a view of man as discarnate mind. But man is not essentially mind, as viewed by idealism, nor special organism, as viewed by naturalism. He is, rather, "a dynamic agent, acting in response to the call of God in the existential context of life." Idealist and naturalist education, although in principle autonomous, always lapse into heteronomy. Estranged from theonomy—finding one's center in God—modern man staggers "back and forth between a heteronomy against which he revolts and an autonomy he cannot bear." Biblical realism, however, knowing man in the heights and depths of his existence, provides him with a center, and offers him the intellectual and spiritual resources to cope with the ambiguities of his life. Will Herberg believes that life should be integrated at all levels by common categories. What he has done in this essay, therefore, is to define the nature and meaning of education in terms congenial to and springing from Biblical faith, in an effort "to bring this important enterprise of the human spirit under the command, judgment, and redeeming grace of God."

Will Herberg is Graduate Professor of Philosophy and Culture in Drew University.

Will Herberg
Biblical Realism as a Norm

I THINK IT WILL BE AGREED THAT EVERY MAJOR PHILOSOPHY of education reflects an underlying anthropology, or "image of man," and is to be understood in its terms. At bottom, there are three basic anthropologies, each defining the *humanum,* "humanness," what it means to be a human being, in a different way. These three "images of man" may be conveniently labeled the *idealist,* the *naturalist,* and the *Biblical-realist.*

Abridged from "Toward a Biblical Theology of Education," *The Christian Scholar,* Vol. 36, No. 4 (December, 1953). Reprinted by permission of the National Council of the Churches of Christ in the U.S.A. and the author.

1. *Idealism.* In the idealist view, man is a mind, immortal and divine, contained in a mortal and earthly body. The *humanum,* the "real" man, is the soul, or mind, or reason, and man's proper life is the contemplative life of the soul.

2. *Naturalism.* In the naturalist view, man is a special kind of organism reacting to, or interacting with, an environment. The *humanum,* the "real" man, is the total organism, and man's proper life is the reactive (or interactive) life of growth and adjustment.

3. *Biblical realism.* In the Biblical-realist view, man is a dynamic agent, acting in a situation in response to the call of God which comes to him in the existential context of life. The *humanum,* the "real" man, is the total person as a willing, deciding, acting being, and man's proper life is the responsive and responsible life of action.

Each of these anthropologies has its own congenial and appropriate philosophy of liberal education. The common premise is that the purpose and end of liberal education is somehow the realization of the *humanum,* the actualization of man's "humanness," but each understands this in a different way.

1. *Idealism.* Since man's "essence," in the idealist view, is understood as mind or reason, the actualization of his humanness is necessarily to be achieved through the proper exercise of this power. "Through the exercise of reason," says Ibn Sina, the distinguished Muslim philosopher, here speaking for all Greek-minded medieval thinkers, "that which is potential within the soul reaches actuality." [1] The proper exercise of reason is, of course, the discovery and contemplation of truth, more specifically the discovery and contemplation of eternal and intrinsic ideas, ideals, and values. Education is thus a *paideia,* a self-cultivation, designed to bring about an inner harmony of the soul under

the kingship of reason. It is surely obvious how neatly this view fits in with the dominant tradition of liberal education; indeed, liberal education as we know it in the Western world grew out of the Greek-idealist view of man and has continued through the centuries to be interpreted and developed in basically Greek-idealist terms.

Greek, too, though somewhat earlier, is the conception of liberal education as the education of the free citizen; that also has passed into Western tradition, though it has taken many forms, reflecting the changing structure of society. Such a concept commends itself to most of us, yet it should be recognized that if that is all liberal education is, its goal is obviously a civic totalitarianism, the total absorption of the individual in the *polis,* in and through which, and never outside of which, he is to realize his humanness. "Greek rationalism," as Hajo Holborn points out, "had no organ for the free individual." [2] Greek thought, in fact, never achieved the concept of the *person*: man was conceived of either as a citizen, totally encompassed in the *polis,* or as a discarnate mind liberated from the "flesh," whether bodily or social, and removed from all time, place, and circumstance. Both conceptions have entered in different proportions into the Greek-idealist tradition of liberal education.

2. *Naturalism.* The naturalist philosophy of education is fairly recent, although it has earlier anticipations. Since man is "essentially" an organism reacting to an environment, both natural and social, the actualization of his humanness, in the naturalist view, is to be achieved through a proper adjustment to that environment. This adjustment is, of course, to be dynamic in view of the constantly changing relations between organism and environment, and so the goals of naturalistic education are characteristi-

cally given in such terms as "growth," "maturation," and "development." Liberal education, in this view, is designed to confer the skills and knowledges necessary for the kind of life appropriate to the very special organism known as man. The skills of social or group living rank high in contemporary naturalistic educational theory and practice.

3. *Biblical realism.* In the Biblical view, man's "essence," if that term can be properly used in such a connection, is his responsive relation to God, his capacity, in freedom and decision, to hear and answer the call of God that comes to him in his situation. Man's essence is thus active, not contemplative; it is related to his "heart" (will, decision), rather than to his "mind": here the Biblical view differs from idealism. But man's essence is also his freedom, and therefore it is somehow nature-transcending and nature-transforming: here the Biblical view differs from naturalism. Man is neither a discarnate mind nor merely an organism: he is a free, responsible person, created in the "image of God." (It might be noted that though the Biblical view differs from both idealism and naturalism, it seems to be further removed from the former than from the latter, for whereas man is in some sense an organism, it is hard to see in what sense he ever is, or can be, a discarnate mind.)

The actualization of man's humanness, which is the end or purpose of liberal education, is, in the Biblical view, to be achieved through achieving a right relation to God, more concretely through loving obedience to God in responsible action in the world, which of course means in responsible action toward one's neighbor. Man actualizes the image of God in which he is made insofar as he loves God with all his heart, with all his soul, with all his might, and his neighbor as himself, and manifests this love in action.

Man's normative life as man is not the contemplation of truth or a proper adjustment to his environment; it is obedience to God through responsible concern for his neighbor. If liberal education is to have any justification at all in the Biblical view, its justification can only be in terms of how it serves this end.

The problem may be posed in another way. One of the primary purposes of liberal education, in the Greek-humanist view that has become traditional in our thinking, is to free the mind of man. Man's mind is held to be enslaved by ignorance, benightedness, the tendency to take illusion for reality (recall Plato's Myth of the Cave); it is thus the purpose of education to dispel ignorance and illusion, to bring the mind to the vision of truth, and in this way to liberate it. Liberal education in the familiar sense seems particularly appropriate for this purpose. But in the Biblical view, man (not his "mind" but his total self) is held to be enslaved not by ignorance but by sin; his plight is not that he is imprisoned in the shadow world of the empirical and time-bound, but that he is under the bondage of idolatrous self-will. Freedom, in this view, means breaking through the vicious circle of self-enclosed idolatry and returning to a God-centered existence. But how can liberal education in the common acceptance of the term help accomplish that?

The dilemma confronting us is now apparent: liberal education is deeply rooted in the idealist and humanist traditions; yet if it is to be affirmed by the man of Biblical faith, it must somehow be brought to make sense in terms of the Biblical-realist view of God, man, and the world. Is that possible? Can liberal education be grounded in the categories of Biblical faith and justified in their terms?

The Bible itself knows nothing, or virtually nothing, of

liberal education in our meaning of the term. Christians and Jews, insofar as they were interested in liberal education at all, thought of it in the familiar rationalist and idealist terms and quite as a matter of course refrained from any attempt to bring it into harmony with the presuppositions of their faith. Reflecting the duality of the Western heritage, they lived in two spiritual worlds—Biblical-Hebraic in religion, Greek-idealist in thought, education, and culture. And so it is, by and large, today, except that the Biblical-Hebraic element has grown even weaker and more unfamiliar.

From the point of view of the man of Biblical faith, this dualism must appear intolerable. One cannot be said to live one's faith unless one tries to understand and deal with all aspects of life in its terms. Is this possible in the field of liberal education?

Liberal Education in a Biblical Framework

It seems to me that a fruitful approach to this question is possible along a way the relevance of which may not appear at first sight. Let us ask the question, What is the place of Job or Ecclesiastes in the Bible? The Bible, in normative Jewish-Christian faith, is primarily *Heilsgeschichte*, the history that reveals and bears witness to God's redemptive dealings with man and that therefore provides the believer with his own authentic "inner history." Neither Job nor Ecclesiastes has any part in the *Heilsgeschichte;* yet these books have their part, an essential part, in the Bible? Why?

Is it not because they constitute, so to speak, a vertical offshoot from the horizontal line of *Heilsgeschichte* in which man's existential predicament is considered in a

Kierkegaardian "instant" as relevant to all phases of redemptive history from Creation and the Fall to the King-
dom of God? Is it not as if the movement of redemptive
history were stopped for the instant, for man to reflect upon
his condition? There is much in the historical books, in
the Psalms, and in the Prophets, of the same character, but
in Job and Ecclesiastes we have the human predicament
presented to us in consummate existential form, with the
"single one," the concrete, existing person, confronting the
problems of his existence in relation to God, man, and the
world.

It cannot escape us that Job and Ecclesiastes bear a
strong kinship in literary type and form—philosophical
reflections, poetic drama of human destiny—to what has
always been regarded as the major content of the "humanities" in liberal education. In a certain sense, they
seem, at least in form, to be more Greek than Biblical:
Ecclesiastes reads like the reflections of a Greek philosopher
of a particularly skeptical and pessimistic kind, while Job
has actually been rearranged several times in the form of
a Greek tragedy. Perhaps for this reason, these books may
serve a mediating function in our inquiry. If we keep
these books and the part they play in the Bible in mind, is
it not possible for us to see liberal education, and particularly the so-called humanities, in a new light, in a light that
makes sense in Biblical terms?

I would suggest that the purpose of liberal education is
to give us a more profound insight into the human situation, into man's creaturely existence in the world (in his
alienation from and need for God), and in this way enhance our understanding of, and sensitivity to, the condition and need of our neighbor as well as our own. History,
philosophy, literature, and art may all be seen as con-

tributing to this end, and thus to find a place in an education that sees the actualization of man's humanness as the achievement of a right relation to God and one's fellowmen. In this way, in short, they may find a legitimate place in a program of liberal education Biblically conceived.

The study of pure science, particularly natural science, has frequently been understood, from a religious standpoint, as in effect a contemplation of the works of the Creator: "The heavens declare the glory of God" (Ps. 19:1). We need not quarrel with this interpretation, but we must note that in the psalm referred to, the theme shifts very quickly from the praise of God's "glory" in the physical universe to ecstatic praise of God's "law," "commandments," and "judgments"; the physical universe is obviously brought in to provide a setting for God's exalted majesty in dealing with men. In Greek idealism, the contemplation of eternal and timeless truths for their own sake may be the highest bliss, but not in Biblical faith, which knows no such truths and does not understand man's primary occupation to be contemplative. The study of the natural universe and its laws has its place in a program of education Biblically conceived, but this place is not an autonomous one, self-justified; on the contrary, it too must be related to the *humanum* in man, to his responsive and responsible relation to God and fellowman.

So understood, liberal education has ample room for the cultural legacy of all peoples, however remote from our own religious center, because the cultural legacy of any people is somehow relevant to an understanding of man's humanness; but for that very reason, the literature of the Biblical tradition is central. The thought and culture of the peoples of the world are of the highest value in the educational enterprise, if critically studied, but for critical study some criterion is necessary. And it seems to me obvious, from the standpoint of Biblical faith, that Plato and Aeschylus are to be understood in terms of Isaiah and Job; Confucius and Marcus Aurelius in terms of Paul, rather than the reverse.

So understood, moreover, liberal education is rather *torah* than *paideia,* rather a way of God-centered orientation in the world—that is how Buber translates *torah*: *Weisung,* direction, instruction, way—than a man-centered self-culture of mind or soul. The difference is of great and far-ranging significance.

Some Implications and Consequences

At this point, it might be well to sum up the differences between the three views of liberal education by tracing a number of important implications and consequences for the what, the how, and the why of education. Such an examination will, I think, show profound, though often hard to define differences at every level at which the problem is approached.

In the Greek-idealist view, truth is impersonal, abstract, universal, essentially timeless and placeless, and knowledge the intellectual apprehension of truth. The personal, where it enters, is subtly depersonalized into "idea" or "value," and the historical dehistoricized into "principle." In the naturalistic scheme, knowledge and truth are taken to be warranted assertions about matters of fact, the personal is reduced to "reactions" and "adjustments," and the concretely historical dissolved into general "laws" and "regularities." Neither can deal adequately with the personal and the historical because neither possesses the categories for it. The content of education reflects this inadequacy:

it is impersonal even where it deals with persons; it is non-temporal even where it deals with time and history. For the purposes of natural science and certain phases of philosophy, this abstract, impersonal, and unhistorical approach is no doubt essential, but no real understanding of human existence seems to be possible in its terms.

As against both idealism and naturalism, the Biblical approach sees truth in its profoundest sense as incarnated in persons and events, and knowledge therefore as existential insight that emerges in personal "meeting" or encounter. This is at the heart of the "scandal of particularity" with which all authentic Biblical thinking is affected. The great problem of education in the Biblical sense is how to communicate truth which is concrete, particular, personal, and historical in conceptualizing language and categories of thought. Dr. Casserley has raised and dealt with this problem most creatively in his profound work, *The Christian in Philosophy*, to which I here refer.

Education in the idealist sense is essentially intellectual contemplation and apprehension; it is therefore again objective and impersonal. The actual techniques and procedures may, and often do, involve dialogue and discussion, but there is no real personal engagement because what is to be learned is not personal or historical. In naturalistic education, learning is basically perhaps even more impersonal, for it is conceived as a matter of stimulus and response, of the molding of the environment, of ongoing experimentation. In the Biblical view alone is education really a matter of personal engagement and existential confrontation. Human being is held to be in its very nature dialogic; it emerges only in a responsive I-Thou relation, first with God and then with fellowman. Human being is also historical; its very texture and substance is activity in time. It follows, therefore, that knowledge that really touches the *humanum*, the humanness of man, can be properly communicated not through the abstract concept but through the living word and deed, and that means personal engagement and commitment. Whether, and to what degree, that is possible in a highly institutionalized educational process constitutes a fundamental problem. It is, however, clear that unless some sort of personal engagement and commitment is achieved, there can be no real education of humanness in the Biblical sense.

Idealist and naturalist education is in principle autonomous, although as we shall soon see it is always lapsing into heteronomy. Man, or mankind, is thought of as essentially self-contained and self-sufficient; the *humanum* that is to be actualized through education is its own end, though frequently this *humanum* is conceived as going beyond the individual and being truly embodied in some collective or corporate form. In the Biblical view, of course, this kind of human autonomy, or rather pretension to autonomy, is the root meaning of sin. In the Biblical view, education must be theonomous because the *humanum* of man has no real being except as centered in God; man can therefore understand himself only if he strives to understand his God-relationship, which is in fact the reality of his *humanum*. It is not that idealist education, or even naturalist education in most of its forms, "disregards" God; on the contrary, God is given his "place," but that place, however important, is something peripheral and subsidiary to man's understanding of himself (and the world). In education Biblically conceived, however, God is at the center because there is no man, or even thought of man, without God. Plato's "Mathematics is the royal road to knowledge" and Pope's "The proper study of mankind is man," reflecting as they do the two sides of liberal education (pure science, the humanities) are to be contrasted with the Biblical "The fear of the Lord is the beginning of wisdom." Idealist and naturalist education is, each in its own way, a song of praise to man: "Glory to Man in the highest, the Maker and Master of all." Education in the Biblical sense, however, is a *laus Deo*, a laudation of God and glorification of his name. It is indeed a process of "taking captive every thought and bringing it into subjection to God" (II Cor. 10:5).

"Heilsgeschichtliche" Orders and the Problem of Education

What has preceded has been, by and large, an attempt to define the place, purpose, and function of education in the order of creation, that is, in the order of things which God created and found good. It is in that sense an effort to establish the normativity of the educational enterprise. But the order in which we live is by no means the order of creation in its original rightness; it is the order of creation "spoiled," upset, perverted, transformed by sin—which is our propensity to make ourselves, our ideas, interests, and concerns, the center of the universe and to comprehend the meaning of all things in their terms, while exploiting every advantage for their aggrandizement and the establishment of our self-sufficiency against God. Sin, in this radical, comprehensive sense, enters and affects education on every level. A full analysis can hardly be attempted, but some aspects of this process may be indicated.

1. Because man, in his sinful egocentricity, finds himself at odds with God and the world, the unity of knowledge and the wholeness of truth are no longer real for him. The truth that he knows is of many kinds, by no means always

concordant; the knowledge that he deals with seems possessed of some inner force of disruption: it is always flying apart, with the fragments each claiming an autonomous existence and the right to define the truth from its own standpoint and in its own terms. To deal with this chaos of centrifugal autonomy, which beyond a certain point makes life literally unlivable, men have been perennially tempted to try to bring about cultural integration through an external and therefore heteronomous unity in which some particular idea or interest is set up as the universal criterion of meaning and truth. As has become evident under totalitarianism, such heteronomy may mean the destruction of everything significant in culture and the conversion of the educational process into a technique of mental and spiritual *Gleichschaltung.*

We are here confronted with a really desperate dilemma. Having lost his center in God, man is always staggering back and forth between a heteronomy against which he revolts and an autonomy he cannot bear. The cultural crisis of our time is particularly revealing. Modern man fought hard and confidently to throw off the ecclesiastical-scholastic heteronomy of the later Middle Ages; he triumphed, and in the eighteenth and nineteenth centuries finally established his intellectual autonomy against God and the world. But this autonomy, once achieved, he has found to be an intolerable burden, something beyond the power of mere flesh and blood to bear. And so he plunges frantically into new heteronomies as expressed in the totalitarian cults of our time. There seems to be no way out of the vicious circle because there is no apparent way of restoring the original wholeness of knowledge and truth. This plight is reflected not only in the institutions of education and culture, but in the soul of man itself.

The fragmentation of knowledge and the decomposition of truth have become a scandal even to the modern mind, and so there are everywhere demands for a restoration of the "unity of principle and practice" on some generally acceptable basis. But is there such a basis short of a theonomous grounding in God, which sinful man in history has never, least of all perhaps in our time, been ready to accept? Shall we try to establish this unity in terms of democracy or reason or the scientific method? However valuable these things are, they are not ultimate and the attempt to effect a unity of culture in their terms can be nothing short of idolatrous.

But the lack of "unity of principle and practice" is not therefore something to which we can become easily reconciled. It reflects the disruption in human thought and existence brought about by man's alienation from God. But for that very reason, it cannot and will not be finally overcome until the final redemption of all life and thought at the "end." No heteronomous unity will do; it will only, and properly, set off a new struggle for autonomy. Theonomy alone can bring unity to the human spirit and provide the *humanum* in man with a secure rootage, but theonomy is an eschatological not a historical possibility. It is a vision, a promise, a demand; it is an ever-relevant principle of criticism and judgment; but it is not something that can find enactment or fulfillment in historical institutions.

And so in our educational enterprise as in our thinking generally, we must recognize but never accept the fragmentation of knowledge and truth. In order to deal with reality at all, we develop organizing and unifying principles of thought and set up structures of intelligibility; these are the presuppositions of science and knowledge about which there has been so much discussion recently. We cannot do without them since presuppositionless thinking is impossible and some unity is necessary if anything is to be known at all. But we must never lose sight of the partial and provisional character of our presuppositions and principles or attribute to them any final and absolute validity, not even to the presuppositions and principles of our Biblical *Weltanschauung*, for even the Biblical *Weltanschauung* is a human *Weltanschauung* and not to be simply identified with God or this truth. To hold the balance in this way between a chaotic relativism and a premature absolutism is no more easy in education and thought than it is in the field of moral action, but it is just as necessary. It means to recognize that presuppositional diversity is inescapable, something that is not always acknowledged by the secular university any more than it is by the religious-sectarian institution; but it also means to recognize that this diversity represents a disruption of the wholeness of knowledge and truth in the order of creation.

2. The operations of sinful egocentricity in the life of thought and culture are perhaps best seen in the ever-present tendency to make of our culture and knowledge an instrument of spiritual self-sufficiency and an idolatrous ground of security and meaning. The old theologians understood the human heart very well when they associated the *libido sciendi,* the lust for knowledge, with other less reputable lusts. What they were saying was what Karl Jaspers meant when he recently spoke of philosophy as being "man's self-aggrandizement through thinking" and what Bertrand Russell had in mind when he gave it as his opinion that "the pursuit of knowledge is mainly actuated by the love of power." The love of power, a primary manifestation of sinful egocentricity, indeed insinuates it-

self into the most sublime and exalted of human enterprises: What is the philosopher's desire to "comprehend
the universe" if not, at least in part, a highly sophisticated
form of the urge to play the God that is found in every
human breast? These considerations are not, of course, to
be taken as an argument for the cessation of thinking; we
are called to creative activity in all fields by our vocation
under God, and, besides, one cannot overcome idolatry by
eliminating that which tends to be idolized, or else the entire world would have to be destroyed. These arguments
are rather an indication of the perilous ambiguity of our
position in the world of thought as in the world of action.

3. Education may become an instrument of power and
self-glorification in another and more obvious sense, in its
impact on social life. Mark Twain is reported to have defined education as the defense of the older generation
against the younger, and no one can deny that there is
profound truth in this witticism. In all education, there is
inescapably an element of domination on the part of the
generation that does the educating over the generation
that is being educated. The German theologian and educator, Oskar Hammelsbeck, pointed to this ambiguity.
"The Scylla and Charybdis of the educational problem in
this respect," he said, "is that the young are not free if
participation in the cultural heritage is withheld from
them, while they are likewise not free if they have no protection against the culture and education forced upon them
(by the older generation)." Just as it can become a weapon
in the "struggle of the generations," so education can become an instrument in the social struggle. We know very
well, even in our own country, the class power of culture
and education. It is no solution to send everyone to college,
although the movement to extend educational opportuni-

ties is certainly to be welcomed. The Education and culture will always be matters of differential attainment, and men will always be prone to exploit these differences, conventionally certified, for their own advantage. This too must never be lost sight of in any overall view of education.

4. A very grave corruption that the cunning of sin introduces into education is the utilization of education itself as a way of evading responsibility. When education is depersonalized and objectified, as it more or less must be as soon as it is institutionalized whatever be the philosophy behind it, knowledge and culture become external, something to be possessed, enjoyed, utilized, rather than something that brings with it a call to commitment and decision. Sir Walter Moberly has noted that "most students go through our universities without ever having been forced to exercise their minds on the issues that are really momentous." This is not merely the fault of curriculum or teaching methods; it is, at bottom, a protective device that irresponsible man—and we are all irresponsible, insofar as we are all sinful—elaborates to externalize and objectify his knowledge and so to keep at a safe distance the call to commitment that comes to him through what he learns and knows. Students often fail to "exercise their minds on issues that are really momentous" primarily because when these issues emerge in the course of education, students—like teachers, like all of us—almost automatically and quite unconsciously devitalize them by turning them into knowledge to be learned or culture to be enjoyed, with no claim upon them or relevance to their existence. Education thus becomes, as I have said, a way of avoiding responsibility. This seems to me to be the most subtle peril to which education is exposed in this our sinful existence.

None of these underlying ambiguities and ambivalences

of the educational enterprise can be taken account of, or dealt with, by the idealist and naturalist philosophies of education. Neither understands the condition of man or has any real sense of his predicament.

Biblical realism understands man in the full dimensions of his being, in his "grandeur" and his "misery" alike. It is thus able to see the full significance of man's capacity for self-transcendence and the indeterminate possibilities of his freedom without imagining for a moment that his freedom is unlimited or that his self-transcendence ever fully escapes the involvements of the self. It knows him as an animal that is more than an animal and as a spirit that is less than divine. It knows him in his creatureliness, his particularity, and his sin; it knows him for what he was created and for what he has made of himself by his willful alienation from God. It knows him in the heights and depths of his existence. It can therefore fully appreciate the painful ambiguities to which he is exposed at every level of life, and provide him with the intellectual and spiritual resources with which to cope with these ambiguities without succumbing to the illusion that he can ever escape from them entirely in the course of his historical existence. This understanding and these resources are surely as necessary in the field of education as in every other area of life.

CHAPTER 11

Christian Ethical Community
as a Norm

EDITOR'S INTRODUCTION

The university as an intellectual, social, and moral community
has disintegrated. Sadly, but finally nevertheless, many educators who acknowledge the truth of that statement go on to
assert that the university cannot again be a community: it is
too large, too diverse, too uncommitted. A college or university might again become a community, however, Waldo
Beach maintains, by sharing obedience to the love of God. On
the intellectual level this would mean shared trust that there is
ultimate meaning in the mystery and a shared sense of the
provisional in the little parts of it that its members grasp. At
the social level, the recovery of community would become
visible in the common allegiance to the well-being of the
others. The intellectual and social aspects would come together in the "niches and crannies of the system where men
find reconciliation to the order of truth and to each other."

*Waldo Beach is Professor of Christian Ethics in The Divinity
School, Duke University.*

Waldo Beach

Christian Ethical Community as a Norm

THIS ESSAY IS AN ATTEMPT TO ASSESS THE QUALITY OF THE American university today as measured by the Christian ethical norms of community.

In common American imagery there is an aura of sanctity hovering over the university campus. It is a blessed place. There seems to be an almost unlimited trust of Americans in the benefits of higher education, as witnessed by the billions poured from federal and private funds into the vast building programs of the universities and the bustle with which every small city sets up its community college. No one without a college education can really presume to belong, to be inside. The subtle processes of ranking and status, in the business and political world, may be made more on the basis of the quality of a man's alma mater than of his home or his church. It may not be too much to say that the campus has surpassed the home and the church, in the American's value scale, as the institution which is trusted as the savior of society, the paradigm of perfect community, where youth are all trained to intelligent maturity and gracious living.

Abridged from "Christian Community and the American University," by Waldo Beach, *Emory University Quarterly*, Vol. XXIII, No. 2 (Summer, 1967). Reprinted by permission of the author and *Emory University Quarterly*.

Yet on occasion this aura of sanctity is jarred, if not shattered, by an explosion. The riots at Berkeley troubled the American dream about the idyllic university with a sudden nightmare. The Easter bacchanalias on Florida beaches are somewhat less genteel than the sober proprieties of June baccalaureates. The widespread use of narcotics and hallucinogenic drugs does not seem to give sign of intelligent maturity. A glimpse behind the ivy-covered walls into a dormitory bull session reveals something less than an eager passion for learning or responsible and considerate student self-government.

While universities expand apace and enrollments soar, there is widespread soul-searching among educators about the inner failure of nerve that besets the university culture. The most bothersome questions are the issues of this present study: What are the terms of authentic community that make a university *one*? Is its trouble a case of lost or mistaken identity? What factors conspire to tear the fabric of community, and what forces are at hand to restore it? Such questions lead beyond purely technical considerations and matters of educational philosophy into moral and, in the last analysis, theological issues.

The Disintegration of the American University

Critics and diagnosticians of higher education in America may display something of the same nostalgia for the Golden Days of the past as the urban sociologist may have for the simple beauties of country life, or church historians for the "pristine purity" of the early church. They forget that the Golden Days were never really that golden. Any memories of a simple unity of the medieval European university, or of an eighteenth-century Harvard Yard where all was peaceful intellectual unanimity, obscure, in the gentle haze of hindsight, the tensions and controversies that no doubt erupted. But by contrast to the contemporary university, there *was* a high degree of intellectual unity in a commonly shared world view. To go back only a century or so in American higher education, if one examines the curriculum of the liberal arts college in New England, one finds a close unity of subjects in classics, natural sciences, English, etc., with a senior "integrative" course in moral philosophy, taught by the president of the college, a churchman and theologian. The currency of intellectual exchange was that of Protestant Christianity. The chapel was at the architectural and emotional center of the campus, where the spiritual and moral purposes of higher learning were celebrated in common worship. No doubt the faculty meetings, however prayerful, were ridden with political in-fighting. No doubt the intellectual waters were not always calm. But the strong sense of identity in a Christian world view gave the original college a high degree of integrity of mind.

The complex story of the shift from this unified college of a century ago to the "multiversity" of today is a familiar one. The gradual change from the authority of theology to the authority of science, the proliferation of the curriculum in the "free elective" system, the multiplication of professions for which the university prepared its students, the religious and ethnic pluralism in the American college population—and the sheer bulk of numbers of students— have all had their disintegrative effect. The end result has been the multiversity, with a curriculum splintered into fragments, where the relation of courses to each other is only one of "simultaneity and juxtaposition," as William Temple noted, and where faculty find no common meeting ground of shared intellectual premises but can talk only with those in their own field. One of its sharpest critics, Robert Hutchins, defined the university as a group of buildings and schools that share a common heating plant.

This fragmentation of a structured body of truth into scattered truths which bear no organic relation to each other: here is the anarchy, the anomie of the modern huge American university, copied in the small college.

Anomie on campus, Hutchins described thus: "The crucial error is that of holding that nothing is more important than anything else, that there can be no order of goods, and no order in the intellectual realm, that there is nothing central, nothing peripheral, nothing primary, nothing secondary, nothing basic, and nothing superficial. The course of study goes to pieces because there is nothing to hold it together." [1] The purported community of scholars united in a common search for truth is splintered into departments and schools, each in political and ideological rivalry with all others, each suspicious of the intellectual credentials of any discipline but its own.

So anomie, pride, and myopic vision pervert the purposes of the university. And the psychological consequences are the moods of alienation and apathy in the motivations that guide faculty and student. The image may be that of the teacher-scholar engrossed in disinterested research or leading the eager student by the hand into the spacious Temple of Wisdom. The reality is somewhat different. Professionalism of the system perverts research into the frantic publish-or-perish grind. The teacher is compelled by the system to stretch each student onto the Procrustean bed of the course requirements. The student, on his part, is alienated from the pursuit of truth into a melancholy apathy, from which he will be prodded only by the requirements of the system to study for grades, to pass courses, to do enough to get through. The disciplines intended to lead the student to responsible maturity in truth-seeking to a considerable degree may thwart that end. The idolatry of grades may require the sacrifice of honor, where to stay in the game, the student may be forced by the system to cheat on exams. So the congenial community of scholars is turned into the competitive society of pedants and operators, in endless anxious skirmishes and political battles with each other.

To be sure, this dark picture is overdrawn and should quickly be corrected by the acknowledgment that there is much eager learning and exciting teaching going on, that the various programs for integration are healthy moves toward wholeness of mind. But in the broad overview, the vital experiments and the integrative efforts go against the main drift of things.

The second form of disintegration of the university is *social*, in the living relationships of its members. Unlike the European university, which bears responsibility for academic relations only, from the start the American university has been a resident community where some outer terms of community relations have to be set. The dominant pattern set by the older college, of course, was the authoritarian paternalistic model of the home, where the college, acting *in loco parentis*, prescribed carefully the rules of behavior for the children in its care. Close community controls by deans and a bevy of housemothers, it was hoped, would protect virginity and cultivate Christian propriety. Chapel was the sign of the presence of a divine chaperon and monitor. The limited size of the student body was itself a social control and gave each student a sense of accountability, for he was known and watched by his peers, if God should not be looking.

Quite the opposite situation prevails in the contemporary university. Partly this is the consequence of sheer numbers. In a university of thirty thousand students, the individual is frightened and lost. There is an inverse ratio between density of mass and a sense of personal identity. Known by no one, the individual feels anonymous. He rushes from circle to circle, hunting for his "real self." More often than not he remains desolate. The incidents of student suicides and the number of psychiatric counseling cases, while of no greater ratio than in society at large, are still shattering to any blissful image of "bright college years."

Community depends also on vital, trusted communications. When a campus becomes too large, the communication among its segments breaks down from what Kenneth Boulding has called the Brontosaurus principle. It becomes too big to cope with itself.[2]

The moral disintegration of the campus is as much due to anomie within as to mass of numbers without. The crisis in community here is that there are no accepted terms of political authority, no common norms of diverse rights and obligations for the various components, faculty, administration, and students. "There is no King in Israel." The paternalistic pattern of authority has been gradually eroded. A nervous administration may be tolerant and permissive, partly to cultivate student responsibility, but more out of considerable moral uncertainty as to what *are* indeed proper modes of campus behavior. The bewildered faculty avoid dealing with the problem of student behavior and pass by on the other side. It is none of their business.

On their part, students are in revolt against paternalism, against conventional standards, against the phony strictures of their parents or any authoritarian figure, in a widespread seething rebellion. But their rebellion gives mark of the same anomie which is one ingredient in the administration's permissivsness. Students are rebels, but often with no cause beyond protest itself. They want a larger voice in setting the terms of social relationships, but are not at all sure what the obligations are which make the exercise of larger rights viable. The surly vocal minority, where not engaged in prolonged thumb-sucking and navel-gazing, do battle with the Administration or the Dean's office (the Enemy) for setting stupid parietal hours and for its breach of contract in failing to make life more pleasant for the tuition-paying customers.

The student attitude toward morality displays a curious ambivalence: a strict conformity to prevailing fashions of the in-group in dress, mores, morals, and even theological beliefs, and on the other side a kind of "live and let live" tolerance of variant behavior on matters of sex ethics, or smoking pot, or treatment of campus property, reflecting a complete individualism. The college student is morally certain of one thing only: he is not his brother's keeper. Anything goes as long as nobody gets hurt. It may be that anomie accounts for both the intolerance and the tolerance; by strict conformity, by going along exactly with the boys, one may cover over his inner moral confusion, while the tolerance expresses more of an uncertainty of conviction than a respect for conscientious differences.

This picture of the university betrays the slovenly use of the big brush. It is indeed a harsh cartoon that surely should be qualified at many points. Matters are really not all that anomic; the reality is an encouraging and discouraging mixture. In the vast lonely sea of the state campus, here and there students find islands of authentic community. In many progressive colleges, where students *are* given a genuine voice in determining their affairs, they exercise their freedom responsibly. In the very ferment and revolt there is search for new norms and new terms of identity, new wine that must break the old wineskins.

Toward the Recovery of Christian Community

To the university president seeking a road out of chaos to coherence, or to a floundering student asking for one good reason why he should stay with it, the suggestion that there is relevance in the Christian tradition for the problems of anomie and alienation may seem like a quaint archaism. "Back to God" or "Come to Christ" would appear more of an escape from than confrontation with the problems here diagnosed. There is wisdom in this suspicion of an instant cure preferred in the Christian faith. We must be careful in distinguishing a false claim from a true claim to relevance of Christianity to the university.

There are some attempts at keeping the integral university centered in mind around Christian doctrine, most notably in Roman Catholic schools. The scholastic system of truth is here the integrating core. In practice, however, as many Catholic educators concede, the integration is fragile at best: the Thomistic scheme is laid alongside the newer sciences, without genuine inner connection achieved. Another attempt to hold higher education under the control of Christian belief is in the "Bible colleges" of the evangelical and fundamentalist denominations. But these violate the essential ground rules of a university, proscribing the lines of research, teaching by an incredible Biblical literalism, and attempting to rest too much on too narrow a base. To require the teacher of psychology or sociology to conform his subject matter to the Lordship of Christ is to violate the integrity of his discipline and to subject universality of truth to parochial dogma.

We would maintain that such attempts at reintegration around any prescribed body of Christian truths, however earnest and pious, do not provide viable answers to the university question. Its likely impact on an intelligent faculty member or student is to encourage duplicity and foment legitimate rebellion. In this sense we would concur with the statement of the Harvard Report on General Education, made some years ago, that "religion is not now for most colleges a practicable source of intellectual unity."[3]

But there is quite another way to approach the problem of intellectual chaos. It has to do with the loves of the heart rather than the sight of the mind, with motivation and stance of spirit in teaching and research and study, rather than with true or false conclusions. In the life of its mind, the members of a university community may be made *one* out of many, integrated out of chaos, by a shared obedience to the love of God. The intellectual form of the love of God does not mean subscription to any creedal statement about the nature of God or his action in history. It means rather a reverence in the face of mystery, a trustful curiosity, a restless searching, doubting, affirming spirit of wonder, sustained by the tacit confidence that there is an order of truth beyond and within the manifold puzzle of the present disorder. As put by H. Richard Niebuhr: "Love to God is conviction that there is faithfulness at the heart of things—unity, reason, form and meaning in the plurality of being."[4] This is the shared faith that makes an assembly of scholars into a community, beneath their plural traditional religious persuasions and the strife of schools and systems that constitute the dynamics of the university's daily life. The scholar coming out of the Roman Catholic tradition might phrase this conviction by affirming that the order of being and the order of value are one. A Protestant way of putting it would be to say that men are justified, as an intellectual community, by the trust of their hearts that there is meaning in the mystery, and that their scholarly work is a response to grace. Even the agnostic, the radical questioner, shares in this community of faith, at least in the sense that he must presume an order of truth for his very questioning of it to be intelligible.

A most important implication of this understanding of the responsible love of God in the life of the mind is for epistemology, or the perennial question of how we know. One basic force that appears to divide the mind of the campus is the so-called split between faith and reason, producing the division between the faithful and the faithless. "Faith" is often taken to mean blind assent to a body of dogma, the stance of the religious man. "Reason" is taken to mean everything that goes under the heading of "scientific method," a critical, cautious, experiential approach to data, where everything must be confirmed by experiment and testing. By such a division in method, of course, the theologian cannot really talk with the scientist on campus, since they do not agree about the basic rules of the hunt.

This stark dualism between faith and reason is false. In every major discipline of study, both faith *and* reason operate together. In the sciences, faith operates as primal assumption or hypothesis on which critical investigation proceeds. All investigation and analysis, microscopic or macroscopic, of enzymes or galaxies is faithful thinking, sustained by a trust that there is an intelligible order in the phenomena studied. Likewise, good theological thinking is not blind credulity, but self-critical, scrupulous in its treatment of evidence and the laws of thought, alert always to check its tenets against experience. So, as much in theological as in scientific reflection, there is faithful reasoning and critical faith. For theologian as much as for scientist or philosopher, doubt is not the foe but the friend of understanding. For doubt keeps faith from credulity, as trust keeps reason from skepticism. The explicit appreciation of this basic ground rule in the community of learning would do much to overbridge the gulf between the sciences and the humanities, and provide an epistemological reconciliation. In this spirit, all members of the university would share in that openness and tentativity which is the wisdom of "scientific method." All parties to the dialogue might concur with the judgment of a seventeenth-century divine that "man hath but a shallow sound and a short reach and deals only with probabilities and likelihoods." Yet a person of intellectual contrition before God is not the radical skeptic or nihilist. He is as trustful that there is ultimate meaning in the mystery as he is distrustful and provisional in his claim for the little part he grasps.

The relevance of theology in recovering community of mind in the university is not, then, by attempting to restore her as queen of the sciences, but by seeing her as servant. In this role, theology is not so much a separate subject in the curriculum—though it is legitimately that—as it is a certain dimension of all subjects. It should bother each classroom—from mechanical engineering to metaphysical poetry—with the great questions of the meaning of human existence. It should haunt each finite truth with the intimations of infinity. It should point each fact, each person, each event, beyond itself to a universal community. Out of this love of God, the members of the scholarly community can serve each other by mutual limitation in a system of checks and balances in a democracy of learning. The scientist, observing rigor and exactitude, may correct the religion teacher's fuzziness, while the teacher of religion may serve the scientist by raising the questions about ends for means, or the moral uses of the power of technology, questions which technology is powerless to answer itself. So some deep sense of interdependence may restore community among students of independent disciplines.

Social Reconciliation

We have traced earlier above the *social* disintegration and anomie of the university, the breakdown of the traditional structures of paternal authority and the revolt of students. What relevance does Christian love have to this perplexing aspect of the university's social life? Again, as with the problem of its disintegration of mind, we set aside the quick remedies of Religious Emphasis Week or the simple prescriptions of the evangelist. But there is an indirect relevance of the great commandment that might be traced out, which provides guidelines for social reintegration.

The university community is not, of course, a community of merely intellectual transaction; it is a community of total persons. Like all communities, it exists in precarious equilibrium between the centrifugal and centripetal thrusts, between the cohesive pull of loyalty and obligation and the scattering drive for rights and privileges. When the centrifugal drive for rights has no countervailing impulse of obligations, the community flies apart into anarchy. The dominant drive on the American campus is the centrifugal one, the pursuit of rights. Whereas the architectural center of the nineteenth-century campus was the chapel, symbolizing and honoring integrative obligations, the center of the twentieth-century campus is the new Student Union Building, complete with bowling alleys and TV lounges—

dedicated to the cultivation of student privileges and comforts. Many a student comes to the university on the assumption that college education is primarily a privilege and that life there should be so organized as to provide him a maximum of happiness. The chief question he asks, as do his parents, is, Are they nice to me? Do they make me happy?

A Christian counterattack for the recovery of community must be more inward than the devices of the dean's office in setting the outer limits of decent behavior, necessary as these are. No legalism really gets at the problem of social responsibility. The return to community lies by way of the recovery of an inner morale derived from responsible love. What can give a Christian moral tone to the university is the shared allegiance of all its members to the well-being of the others, the common persuasion that each is responsible to God for his neighbor in concern and respect. Responsibility in love provides the cohesive force that reconciles the community from its brokenness and sustains it in trust underneath the inevitable collisions of the interests of its parts and the diffusions of its pursuit of rights.

The university professor, for his part, would discover his Christian vocation or identity in cultivating the personal equation within the cracks of the impersonal system. "He took a personal interest in me." This is one of the tributes that students pay to the memorable teacher. This "personal interest" does not mean the chumminess of the "operator," who seeks first a high rating in the student evaluation poll. The "personal interest" may be exacting and rigorous in its intellectual demands, for Christian love is accountable to God for the neighbor. The authentic teacher's love is sensitive and alert to the whimsies and talents and shortcomings of his student, but not sentimental or soft. The vocation of the Christian teacher, by the terms of the great commandments, is to be the mediator of a sacred order of truth to a sacred order of persons. "Thou shalt love the Lord thy God." This means, in research and writing, in laboratory and classroom, a careful regard for the order of truth, in all its elusive and compelling mystery. "Thou shalt love thy neighbor as thyself." This means the teacher's befriending his student as a sacred "thou," infinitely precious.

We speak here, to be sure, in a highly normative vein. How can a teacher have a personal regard for that one student about to knock on his office door when he is teaching sixty of them—his life cluttered with committees, chores, articles overdue, the next class, etc., etc.? The definition of the ideal college in the nineteenth century was "Mark Hopkins on one end of a log and a student on the other," but a twentieth-century Mark Hopkins may be so busy at log-rolling in the political jungle of the university that he never can sit on it and talk with a student. The system seems the implacable enemy of community and personal love an impossible demand. Yet there are niches and crannies in the system where men do find reconciliation, partial though it be, to the order of truth and to each other.

The administration, for its part, is put under obligation by the great commandment to seek to make the "system" it administers instrumental to the good of persons within it. This means that the dean, as with the faculty member, must see the "mature manhood" of the student as the end for which all the regulations should be directed, and for whom if need be they should be abrogated. In the face of a surging student protest and clamor for a larger voice, or for "participatory democracy," the president is by the terms of responsible love required to listen in patience, to sift as best he can the legitimate from the illegitimate claims, to risk extensions of freedoms on the capital of proven student responsibilities, and at the same time to explain his obligations to constituents of the university community—parents, trustees, alumni—other than the students, and to point out that students' demands may not coincide exactly with the students' real needs. This may not avail to satisfy the students, but it will be a stance of responsible love, and it may keep open the lines of trusted communication throughout a controversy.

The student, for his part, may recover his identity in Christian vocation also under the terms of responsible love for God and neighbor. This does not mean a Pharisaic parade of piety or necessarily a public declaration for Christ. It means, in the secret places, a shift of motivation in study from the egocentric to the theocentric. It means that the student sees the university as the place where he may equip himself to fulfill the law of love in service to the larger community.

"Knowledge is in order to goodness." This Calvinistic phrase is pertinent to the issue of the motivation for study. In one sense, surely, the pursuit of truth in the university is disinterested, morally neutral. It is prostituted when turned to any partisan purpose, of church or state. But in another sense, technical knowledge *cannot* be morally neutral, for it is always held as a tool in the hand of a living person who has loyalties and antipathies, loves and hates, who will use his knowledge to serve his causes, be they malevolent or benevolent. Whether the educated person tears or strengthens the fabric of community depends not on the extent of his information but on the sensitivity of his conscience, the bent of his will. His will may be bent inward to himself. He may treat his college education as a rehearsal for the comforts and privileges of status in the affluent society. With such a *voluntas* he will regard his citizenship in the college community as rather a contract whereby his parents pay the college to allow him the pursuit of his happiness. Or his will may be bent outward, by *agape*. He may treat his college as a covenant community of which he is a junior member, so to speak, obliged by the terms of the covenant to study to become, not a parasite or ornament, but a servant of society. For whatever secular profession he trains, this is his Christian vocation.

Now, given the mixture of sin and grace abounding in every empirical university, it is plain that any given student group in any given dormitory could not be sorted into two bins: the pagans of in-turned wills, the saints of outer-turned wills. What is here drawn is more of a psychological than a sociological division. Any single student is at heart a tussle of contrary wills. But one may yet realistically discern, in the moral mixture, preponderant tendencies of will and crucial orientations of purpose. Insofar as the will to learn to serve is predominant, to that degree one may declare the presence of Christian community in that person and on that campus.

What has just been said is put in normative and prescriptive terms. This is not entirely idle moralizing, however, for there is much empirical evidence on campus for a strong student response to the needs of community. By participation in the civil rights movement, or a tutoring program in the Negro ghettos, or a summer work camp project, or the Peace Corps, a student who may have been turned in on himself may be flung out in engagement with desperate human need and led to find himself by losing himself in service to neighbor. His impatience with the staid and cloistered niceties of his courses back on campus and his demand for the *relevance* of the academic to the human situation are a sign of grace, of *agape* in anomie, for they mark his personal search for identification with Christian community.

Chapter 12

A Pluralistic Model

Editor's Introduction

Is there a way of providing for a variety of contrasting, perhaps even conflicting, commitments, while at the same time maintaining the strength and clarity that come with institutional single-mindedness? Since there is no one form or philosophy of undergraduate liberal education but several, and since each has its excellences, is there a way to associate a variety of them without diluting the distinctiveness of any of them? Warren B. Martin, writing both out of his educational researches and his philosophical reflections, believes there is. The cluster college, he argues, provides a unique way to institutionalize both organizational diversity and value diversity.

Warren B. Martin is Coordinator of Development in the Center for Research and Development in Higher Education, University of California, Berkeley.

Warren B. Martin
A Pluralistic Model

CLUSTER COLLEGES OFFER A WAY TO CHANGE AND IMPROVE institutions of learning by giving a new twist to the ancient maxim "Divide and conquer." They may be expected to divide the masses of students into groups small enough to encourage identity and participation, thereby creating, as an additional benefit, a way for the absolute size of the university to increase while the working units remain small. And more, they should help to conquer that student apathy and hostility which grow out of a sense of powerlessness, by encouraging student involvement with the faculty in testing innovations, thus creating in the university a mechanism for institutional change without sacrificing tradition and order.

But more important than any of these reasons for the establishment of cluster colleges is the potential the concept has for the development and testing of holistic alternative models that may prove appropriate for the future of higher education. Changes in the radical model colleges could well follow two tracks—organizational or structural variations and diversity in value orientation. Universities could in these ways test alternatives to the present organizational bureaucracy and value conformity.

Abridged from "The Will to Be Different," by Warren B. Martin, *Saturday Review*, January 21, 1967. Copyright 1967 Saturday Review, Inc. Used by permission of Saturday Review, Inc., and the author.

Admittedly, cluster colleges presently operating are not going as far as is here proposed. They show some interest in achieving organizational distinctiveness but little interest in distinctiveness at the level of values. It is a difference familiar to contemporary organization theory, the difference between changing "the processes *within* the system and the processes of change *of* the system."[1] Three characteristics now typify cluster college programs and they are all concerned with changes in the processes within systems.

Existent cluster colleges, first, have initiated academic innovations which encourage independent study, student-formed seminars, tutorials, modified community government, closer student-faculty working relations, and academic calendar variations. Curriculum revisions such as problem-theme courses, the "three-tier" plan of study, and other action-oriented changes of the conventional ordering of both general education and specialization are also in evidence.

A second characteristic shared by cluster colleges, again with variations, is a residential arrangement in which facilities and programs combine to keep the student in the climate of learning. Faculty studies, seminar rooms and classrooms, even faculty apartments, are often in or near dorms, Oxford and Cambridge style, with the intent to encourage vital academic relationships and aid in the achievement of the spirit of community. The planners believe, with Aristotle, that the happiness of man is best achieved in the life a community. So, all-college activities such as "High Table" dinners or "College Night" are held, not only to enhance the academic and aesthetic contacts but also to encourage community by bringing college personnel together in a shared enterprise.

Another feature of cluster college development is the

concern for some measure of autonomy within the sponsoring university. Actual administrative arrangements vary greatly among institutions, yet wherever these colleges exist there is tension between the necessity for loyalty to the parent institution and the need for freedom to innovate. Such tension is inevitable. Innovations are, after all, explicit or implied criticisms of the *status quo*. Many of the themes emphasized in cluster colleges—identity, relevance, involvement—are those of the systems shakers. The more radical the program, the more the college becomes an attempt to institutionalize anti-institutionalism. And the hazards are as great as the tensions are inevitable. Norman Birnbaum said, "Hell hath no fury like a vested interest scorned." A maxim for innovators as they strive to establish a working relationship with the personnel of the general university might be: Relate to establish confidence, in confidence establish autonomy.

It may be because this issue of autonomy and accountability is so explosive and complex that there is such a dearth of radical thinking in present cluster college planning. Many proposals are hardly more than house plans, ways of handling masses of students so as to minimize impersonality —elaborate recipes most noteworthy for cutting the pie bite-size. Even where more substantial innovations are introduced, the changes are often nostalgic attempts to recapture a lost small-college ethos, and an old liberal arts curriculum. It is almost as though the promoters adopted these themes for no better reason than that these were the sorts of changes faculty might be expected to permit in an ancillary program, as a way of assuaging their guilt for having long since abandoned such emphases in their own departments. Of course there are other and better reasons for the curricula of these small colleges, but there is no denying that political realities compromise the extent of change.

If the creation of small colleges in large universities is to be more than an opportunity for architectural audacity or schemes for the duplication of administrators and the expansion of budgets, if the new colleges are to be innovative at the point of basic university reforms, it is evident that more radical planning is needed. The search for distinctiveness is an invitation to new directions.

Structural Distinctiveness

At the level of organization, alternative college models might well show experimentation in scheduling according to the needs of particular programs, even to the extent of producing calendar variations within a university. There would be secondary benefits. It would then be impossible for comptrollers or registrars or directors of food services to go on doing things in the same old ways. The old ways would not serve the new needs. Necessity is not always the mother of invention, but it may encourage a necessary interest in change.

Could there not be more diversity in grading and evaluating processes? Certain programs might lend themselves best to letter grades, some to term letters, others to a pass-fail arrangement. Could there not also be greater use made of environmental and nonintellective variables in the student selection process? This idea has been tested at Harvard where 85 percent of two hundred young people admitted on the strength of criteria other than high College Board scores graduated. In these and other ways the new colleges could help a university learn that needs vary and that procedures should be appropriate to needs.

There might also be reason to introduce variation in the social contracts that govern student life at the different colleges. Some programs might benefit by living arrangements and social regulations that would be inappropriate for another place or ethos. A pluralistic society should not be surprised by differences in its educational network— even at the levels of hours for women, dating provisions, dress regulations, drinking rules—and all of this at the same university, among its several colleges. In this, the university would be the society in microcosm. Students would get new insights into diversity and learn that privileges are sometimes commensurate with responsibilities.

Most educators today acknowledge the need for changing the quantifying mind-set that has resulted from equating course credits and unit hours with education—and the cluster colleges provide a good opportunity to break with that fixation. Let each college arrange for a unified learning experience according to the objectives and values of the college, and set appropriate graduation requirements. In some programs this might mean a prescribed set of courses; in others, more freedom could be allowed, with students constructing their own programs, and the student work could be evaluated by examination. Because human abilities and interests vary, there is value in such flexibility.

Diversity in the university need not mean anarchy. There could be unifying standards. Although each college would be challenged to authenticate itself through fidelity to its own declared purposes, the quality and relevance of its work in relation to the traditional components within the system could be evaluated through all-university examinations. And other continuing kinds of comparative evaluations could be made: when students from the innovating college take courses in conventional departments in the university, when they transfer to other schools, when they enter graduate and professional programs.

But concern for standards is only one of the reasons given by parent organizations for insisting that offspring colleges conform to established policies and procedures. There are also the arguments of efficiency and convenience. Large size, it is said, necessitates routinized arrangements as a safeguard to sanity. No wonder so many of us are interested in channels rather than change.

But now, in the cluster college concept, we are talking about decentralization and about dividing universities into smaller units. The concept provides an opportunity for functional individuation; furthermore, computers do miracles with minutiae. We are freed by this idea and by technology to examine what the former necessity for organizational uniformity has done to inhibit the quest for alternative models. If the old formulas applied to the new opportunities have a way of making over the new in the image of the old, as we suspect, and if we therefore have reason to believe that it would be better to put the new wine of innovation into new wineskins, then we should not hesitate to challenge the supposition that colleges established within the general structure of existing universities must adhere to the organizational arrangements of the sponsoring body. Both the ends we seek and the means we need may be new ones. The principle for cluster colleges should be that the old way of doing things can always be a guideline but should never be a noose.

The issue of structural diversity in cluster colleges is raised to a new order of importance if we understand that much more than efficiency and convenience are at stake. Organizational differences—curriculum variations, social-academic interrelations, autonomy in governance—are mechanisms by which we encourage the quest of the various colleges for value commitments that will make them identifiable and intensive communities within the large and too often isomorphic university.

Value Distinctiveness

An educational rationale is, of course, always operative in some measure for institutions as well as individuals. Nowhere do we teach just anything; everywhere we show selectivity, taking one thing, rejecting something else. Philosophical norms, consciously or unconsciously espoused, provide the criteria for selection.

Our problem is that most schools have not been characterized by conscious effort in this area; they have not been composed of people who are what Jean-Paul Sartre called "stalkers of meaning." Consequently, the educational philosophy is often determined willy-nilly, by the pressure of external circumstances or disciplinary biases, by hoary tradition or anticipatory opportunism. Again, on other campuses nothing is definite, so nothing is definitive. Without a philosophical framework, faculty and students lack an institutional standard against which to test themselves; and this is a day when faculty need such a standard because they are at the stage of life when, as Erik Erikson put it, the issue is integrity, just as students need it because they are at the stage of life where, as Edgar Friedenberg has shown, the issue is self-identity. And neither faculty nor students can decide such issues in a void.

Too many colleges and universities are characterized by philosophical timidity or vacuity because educators have not been able to demonstrate the superiority of one educational philosophy to another, and they haven't known how to incorporate several philosophies into a given institution without fratricidal warfare. So it has seemed expedient to play down the whole business. They have decided a vacuum was better than a whirlwind.

Now we see in the concept of cluster colleges the possibility of a better solution—a solution that provides for both definition and diversity, for coteries of committed people and for challenges to all commitments.

Research findings at the Center for Research and Development in Higher Education, University of California, Berkeley, support what the history of education suggests, namely, that the vitality of an educational philosophy develops in direct proportion to the meanings it offers and the challenges it faces. The best educational environment is one in which there are both those who say, "We have answers," and those who say, "We have questions." Commitment benefits by criticism, for thus commitment is exercised. Criticism needs commitment; it works only in the context of real alternatives. And creativity needs both. It begins in criticism, yet at the same time, its own validation depends on comparison. Colleges and universities, like persons, can thrive on the tensions of comparison and change if meaning can be assigned to their struggles. Men, like their muscles, go flabby in a tensionless state; but men, unlike body tissue, need meaning as well as movement for social well-being. Thus, our interest is in academic programs with distinctions that matter. Differences that make no difference, William James used to argue, are not differences.[2]

There are not many colleges in America, and almost no state universities, characterized by values so distinctive as to really shape the life of the place. Antioch, Reed, Goddard, Raymond, perhaps Berkeley in recent years, and a few others make contributions at this level, but the paucity of examples is proof of the conformity that underlies the alleged diversity of higher education.

And this is so at a time when Americans, moving into the epoch of automation and cybernation, are groping for goals beyond technology and for a style of life appropriate to new human and social conditions. In this context of radical change, when home and church have lost authority and values are attenuated, there is urgent need for universities to function as centers of independent thinking, committed to opening issues, probing alternatives, and yet also providing programs that stand as "life cores" in the setting of the university's impersonal, philosophically obfuscated, complex organization.

In most universities today the value vacuum at the institutional center and the near anarchy with regard to norms and models everywhere else leave the student either with no definite standard against which to test himself or only the value presuppositions of various departments—unexamined within many departments and often conflicting among departments—out of which to devise some sort of total configurational awareness. The result is an identity crisis for the institution and a disintegrative learning experience for the students.

American universities have encouraged the exploration of ideological alternatives in the classroom. We know how to keep a lot of balls in the air at the same time. But the personal commitments of the faculties and administrators have seemed so malleable or so minimal that students have often concluded that a hierarchy of values is unnecessary or impossible. But a life without distinctions is boring even as one without meaning is death. Men cannot live in a value vacuum any more than they can live in an oxygen

vacuum.[3] We see this now, hence the reaction that is developing to the metaphysical inadequacies of the old
liberalism and the renewed interest in an unapologetic
declaration of suppositions, objectives, and norms. We are
beginning again to see the ubiquity of value judgments,
explicit or otherwise, even as we now concede their provisional nature.

Under the cluster college arrangement we hypothesize,
the university taken as a whole would be heterogeneous,
reflecting the pluralism of society. Individual colleges
within the university might well be organized around, for
example, a curriculum based on humanist classics, or an
educational philosophy keyed to some form of essentialism
or existentialism or analytic philosophy. A program centered on urban problems offered by an institution located
in the city or a college featuring learning by the new
electronic media might be viable contributions.

The idea of cluster colleges also invites the establishment
in the secular university of programs in which the great
religious faiths, East and West, could speak without dilu-
tion or apology to the whole of the student's life. Traditional concepts of the separation of church and state
notwithstanding, perhaps the Roman Catholic or Presby-
terian churches might sponsor a college where, within the
university, the Judeo-Christian teachings, which have fig-
ured so prominently in our history and still hold residual
power in society, would get rigorous study.

Another college might be known for courses conceived
and led by students, which cohered, say, around the study
of political and social radicalism. For such a school, faculty
could be drawn largely from departments elsewhere in the
university when needed to serve as lecturers and resource
persons. This widening and recharging of the university's
curriculum would mean that some of the subjects which

have interested advocates of "free universities" would be studied under the aegis of accredited universities, and that some of the people now alienated because of the blandness of so many course offerings would find involvement and standing in established schools.

Students in universities featuring value-oriented cluster colleges would be able to choose among colleges, each having a special character. Participants in these small schools would be members of a community, in fellowship with those who have made commitments and exercised self-discipline in order to achieve goals that would not otherwise be possible. Yet they would be members also of a large, diversified university.

The student's experiences in the new college would differ from those he would encounter if he studied one or another specialization in this or that department of a more conventional institution. The value commitments of a cluster college would give it institutional character and, since most of a student's work would be done in one college, a large part of his program would be imbued with the educational and social priorities of the school's philosophy of education.

Furthermore, the residential aspect of the cluster college plan provides an opportunity to establish a climate of learning that can carry the values of the program to the student at many levels. Much of a student's learning takes place outside the classroom through various informal encounters. Thus, a college of consequence will offer its students both standards and community.

Community is not possible without standards. And while standards can be imposed without community, they are more easily achieved where community exists. When the educational system does not provide them, the young lapse into apathy or opt for anarchy.

Value-oriented cluster colleges would not exist in isolation, and the perspectives of each program would not go unchallenged. Students would take some courses elsewhere in the university; faculties would have full standing in the larger organization; the diversity of the university would provide options and correctives to the stance of any one college. These would not be cloistered colleges, but the philosophy and structure of each program would be pointed toward making student and faculty learning experiences deeply personal.

Some educators think that making education personal means the creation of a protective society where faculty brood over students as God brooded over his creation. This is oppressive personalization. Others think it is just a matter of mix, or of arranging tracks that bring people into physical proximity to the extent that they are obliged to greet each other as they pass. This is the grunt-as-you-bump approach, and one capable of achieving only perfunctory personalization. But there is a vastly different sense in which education can be personal, and to understand it we should read Martin Buber's essays entitled "Education" and "The Education of Character." There he talks about "inclusion," about getting into a human relationship in which you truly "experience the other side." Buber illustrates: "A man belabours another, who remains quite still. Then let us assume that the striker suddenly receives in his soul the blow which he strikes. . . . For the space of a moment he experiences the situation from the other side." [4] How many of us think about making education personal in this inclusive sense? Most of us know little of such dialogical relationships. In cluster colleges, however, under the terms I have sketched, students and faculty together would be encouraged to achieve it because they would be obliged to ask, "What has meaning for me and what has importance for others?" "How do we develop an ethic of individual honesty and an ethic of social responsibility?" Confronted by the university's diversity, its pluralism and anarchy, they would ask, "What is the basis for authority?" "What do we hold in common?" There are no questions more relevant for our time.

Are we willing to run the risks of substantive diversity? It could mean a radical change for the public university in its relationship to society. If the pressures of constituencies can force private institutions, the "independent" colleges, into an uncritical acceptance of what are thought to be societal norms, it may be even more difficult to establish divergent value options in public universities. Embodying a "service concept" and required to live by the sort of consensus that is necessary to secure a broad base of support, these schools are almost totally mimetic in values. And we seem to prefer it that way.

The problems, of course, would not all be external; there is also the threat of schism within. American institutions of higher learning, despite their historical perspective, scholarly acumen, and collective erudition, may not be sophisticated enough to encourage diversity of basic issues without incurring destructive consequences.

Even if a modest beginning were made, with emphasis put first on structural distinctiveness, allowing ideological distinctiveness to emerge later, as much trouble would be generated from within as from without. Assuming that governing boards were willing to grant autonomy to the cluster colleges, autonomy would not, of course, guarantee innovation. If leaders of the new programs have the same hierarchy of values as those on the old campuses, they will talk of distinctiveness but strive for parity. New colleges may, therefore, project the idea of distinctiveness only as a means for establishing their identity and their budgets, with their eye on the ultimate end of matching their progenitors in size, research, and those other "distinctions" that have recently come under justifiable criticism. Success is measured by standards and, remember, standards are fixed by values. Can the new programs be significantly different if their leadership measures achievement by the old values? Our faith is that *hubris* does yield to the power of a higher affection, as religions have shown, and therefore we may hope that both organizational change and ideological identity will triumph in the cluster colleges.

Clark Kerr has decided that the most serious crisis in higher education is in undergraduate training, particularly of students in general education and those not yet ready to declare a specialization.[5] Roger Heyns, of Berkeley, has argued that lack of agreement on the nature of the university is perhaps our most serious problem.[6] Cluster colleges conceived as alternative models to the dominant learning environment are a means of getting at both issues. Such colleges can yield fruitful responses to these challenges if they are granted sufficient freedom to establish curricula, facilities, and procedures distinguished by the values they have made their own.

This is a way to help youth develop a capacity for judgment, give essence as well as form to the diversity of American higher education, and bring meaning to the experiences of all participants.

Chapter 13

A Singular Model

Throughout higher education today thoughtful educators are searching for ways to respond to cries for relevance, meaningful curriculum, innovation, and community. They are finding responses in those features of higher education traditionally located in Christian colleges when they have been at their best. Yet, paradoxically, at the very time when those characteristics of the Christian college which have made it distinctive are highly prized elsewhere in academe, they have fallen out of fashion in the institutions that formerly claimed them as their hallmarks. A paralysis of nerve inhibits the church-related college from capitalizing vigorously on those features of its academic program that are widely viewed today as important —even essential—to meaningful higher education: smallness and residentiality, institutional commitment, liberal and humane learning, concern for the synoptic meaning of experience, moral seriousness, conviction about the importance of the academic study of religion, and motivation to the service of human good. Editor Averill argues that this is the time in history for the Christian college to perform the things it has long professed.

Lloyd J. Averill is Dean of the Faculty and Professor of Religion and Sociology in Davis and Elkins College.

Lloyd J. Averill
A Singular Model

THE PROTESTANT COLLEGE STANDS JUST NOW AT A CURIOUS juncture in the history of American higher education. On the one hand, there has never been a time in the recent past when the marks that have traditionally been thought to distinguish our Protestant colleges have been so admired by secular educators and secular educational institutions. To be sure, not all of these marks—I shall be noting seven of them—are a direct result of our Protestant ethos, but most of them are; and even those which are not derived from Protestant predilections have been, to some degree at least, influenced by them.

I

(1) Typically the Protestant college has been small and residential. (2) Its identity and unity has derived from a distinctive institutional world view; that is, it has professed an institutional commitment to value the world through Christian perceptions. (3) Its curriculum has been defined primarily by the liberal arts and sciences. (4) It has approached the end of education not simply by prodding the student to a massive accumulation of facts but by aiding him in the creation of a synoptic vision. (5) Its style both of learning and of living has been marked by moral serious-

Originally published in 1969 as *Agenda for the Protestant College.*

ness. (6) It has had a strong conviction about the importance of the academic study of religion. And (7) it has sought to reproduce in its graduates, as it has desired to exhibit in its own life, motivation to the service of human good.

Remarkably and gratifyingly, it is precisely these things which are now being called for by many educators outside our Protestant colleges and universities, and being called for with increasing urgency. Let me cite a few instances from the many that might be listed.

1. One need only name Michigan State University and the University of Massachusetts to be reminded of a growing number of comprehensive state institutions which have begun to develop small residential colleges as significant teaching units within the larger multiplex. Rising interest in the cluster college derives similarly from a concern to give significant visibility to the individual while increasing the capacity of the college to be a genuine community of learning.

2. When it comes to institutional commitment, Dr. Warren B. Martin, of the University of California at Berkeley, has warned that a "value vacuum at the institutional center" deprives the student of a "definite standard against which to test himself." The result, says Dr. Martin, is not only a disintegrative learning experience for the student, but an identity crisis for the institution.[1] John Gardner has recently observed that it is increasingly difficult to identify the modern university. As "industry and government, with their huge research and education programs, come to look more and more like universities," and as "universities with their worldly interests come to look more and more like the rest of society," Gardner thinks the result is that it becomes harder and harder to tell just "what is university and what is non-university."[2] Gardner's ob-

servation alarms economist Walter Adams, of Michigan
State, and English professor Adrian Jaffe, formerly of the
University of Michigan. There is only one way to maintain a clear distinction between university and nonuni-
versity, Adams and Jaffe insist: "[Educational] institutions,
no less than individuals, require a clear sense of identity,
and a commitment to a belief system which can serve as
a blue-print for relating to their environment."[3]   No
church-related college president could put the case for institutional commitment more strongly than have these two
state university scholars.

3. Interest in the liberalizing of education is now per-
meating professional schools even in such traditionally
narrow fields as agriculture and engineering. Paul Miller,
former president of West Virginia University, has recently
chaired a task force for the Committee on the Professional
School and World Affairs, and that experience has led him
to the conviction that professional schools

> must take a greater interest in educating the whole
> man: to impart values, attitudes, sensitivities, and a
> world view of man, institutions, and processes. No
> longer can the professional schools discharge this re-
> sponsibility by requiring the student to take a few courses
> in the humanities and the social sciences.[4]

And rumors are abroad that in the graduate schools, even
in such a discipline-oriented field as psychology, fresh winds
are blowing toward larger interdisciplinary possibilities.

4. What of concern for the synoptic, for the integration
of the often discrete lumps of learning into effective patterns of meaning? Warren Martin, of Berkeley, is quite
frank in saying that the worth of an educational program
is to be measured by the degree to which students and
teachers alike are encouraged to become "stalkers of mean-

ing." Stalkers of facts they will also be, says Dr. Martin, but "whatever the discipline or specialization, they must learn to seek out the deeper meanings—principles, values, goals—and to do this, they must make judgments within the context of some sort of philosophical framework." [5] Columbia historians Hofstadter and Hardy call this quest for larger patterns of meaning "the most vital drama of our times" and express the hope that this quest may "so permeate the college and university that . . . they will help students become the kind of people who realize in their transient existence an eternal meaning." [6]

5. When nihilism grows daily more fashionable, perhaps it is not surprising that sensitive men in all kinds of institutional settings are asking about the role of the academy in moral learning. One of the most impressive advocates of such a role for the church-related college is not himself a member of such a college. Dr. Earl J. McGrath, director of the Institute of Higher Education at Columbia University Teachers College, has recently declared that if the church-related college fails to concern itself with "character and the qualities of personality of which it is composed," its teaching "will become as irrelevant to the basic human problems of our times as that of many of its more prestigious sister institutions already is." [7] Educators in other kinds of institutions fear that irrelevance too. Dean Herbert Stroup, of Brooklyn College, has called upon college counselors to reexamine their broad tolerance even of the most extreme forms of student behavior, lest students "assume that neither the counselor nor anyone else has settled views or convictions regarding ethical behavior." He joins Dean E. G. Williamson, of Minnesota, in urging counselors to abandon their "neutrality" roles and instead "to help the student grow in moral and social ways." [8]

6. Surely the best evidence that the academic study of

religion has found a new acceptability well beyond the church-related college is seen in the astonishing rate at which state-supported schools have been establishing full departments of religion and appointing to them some of America's most distinguished religious scholars. And this development is matched by a growing and widening desire on the part of undergraduates for religious study. When the classes of 1965 and 1966 at Brooklyn College were asked about specific courses of interest to them not offered at that college, there was an almost two-to-one response for courses in religion! [9]

7. And what of a desire to motivate students toward humanitarian service? I dare say that Chancellor John Caldwell, of North Carolina State University, is not alone among educators in state-supported schools when he admires the commitment of students to such ventures as VISTA and the Peace Corps. "Whatever can produce this kind of decision in a student," says Dr. Caldwell,

> may be beyond the purely academic task, but it ushers the intellect into the service of humanity. It may be both different from and more than the counting of course credits, grades, quality points, and prerequisites but not beyond what is worthy of higher education. [10]

II

This recitation of support for the traditionally distinguishing marks of church-related education—support from educators quite outside our church-related institutions—is intended to make a single point. If there is one set of questions that I am most often asked, by teachers and administrators in our Protestant colleges and by others as well, it is this: Does the church-related college have a future? Is it now an educational, and perhaps also a religious, anomaly? Is there any way to justify the continued existence of such institutions? My recitation is intended as an answer. *In my view, there has never been a time in the recent history of American higher education when it was easier to make a case for what the church-related college at its best has traditionally intended to do.* And it is precisely those who have no vested interest in our kinds of schools who are, in effect, arguing that case eloquently for us, as I have just been at some pains to show.

But this is not why the Protestant college now stands at what I called, in my first sentence, a "curious juncture" in the history of American higher education. What is curious, on the other hand, is that *at precisely the time when the case for our kind of education can be made most persuasively, there is too much evidence of a growing loss of nerve within the church-related colleges themselves*—a willingness now to abandon our traditional aims in eager imitation of educational fashions that are, if my evidence is accurate, steadily going out of fashion.

So (1) we drift into uncontrolled growth, with student populations increasingly nonresidential, and give inadequate attention to ways of preserving individuality and community. (2) We attempt to make an educational virtue of philosophical neutrality, partly because we dread the agony of hammering out institutional commitments. (3) Liberal teaching erodes, in spite of nominal distributional requirements, with individual academic departments looking more and more like professional mini-schools interested primarily in reproducing their own specialized kind. (4) With such academic fragmentation, questions of larger meaning or of a synoptic vision can barely be asked, let alone answered. (5) Equivocation on critical moral issues by teachers and administrators, and the enforcement of college regulations in ways that reflect curious moral priorities, are scarcely conducive to moral seriousness in our students. (6) Where the department of religion is notorious for its "gut" courses or its pedestrian instruction, the religious seriousness of the college is similarly compromised. And (7) when it comes to inculcating humanitarian concern, that is perhaps not so much disavowed as ignored. It is not valued highly enough to make it competitive with the compulsion for grades and graduate school supported by sanctions dear to teachers and administrators.

Let it be quite clear that in these remarks I do not claim to draw the profile of the typical Protestant college, and I hope no one will report them as if I had. I am far from suggesting that this is what we all look like. What I have called a failure of nerve is not a universal condition among us. There are presidents and faculties hard at work to preserve the best out of the tradition of Protestant higher education. Nor does the failure of nerve have uniform consequences even where it exists. But that there is evidence of such failure in our Protestant educational effort at too many points to be ignored is a judgment for which I am prepared to take full responsibility, and I have tried to suggest some of the forms in which I observe it.

Perhaps, if what I have said thus far has any truth in it, it may not be brash or presumptuous for a single individual to propose an agenda for the entire Protestant educational enterprise, for the agenda is not, in fact, of my own making. I simply want to remind us all of what we have intended to be at our best, and in the presence of that intention to urge a new institutional self-respect. Nor, I hasten to add, is this simply because our colleagues in other educational enterprises appear to be valuing what we have valued, though that is a welcome development. Rather it is because what we have valued in the past is still valuable, in the full and literal meaning of that word.

Then let me review those seven marks again, for they comprise, so I am persuaded, our urgent agenda.

III

First, smallness and residentiality. College residence halls are not simply arrangements of convenience, nor are they, as our students sometimes allege, instruments of financial extortion and physical torture. The college residence hall is the concrete symbol of a broadened context for learning.

There is no doubt, after all, that men and women between the ages of eighteen and twenty-one will learn a great deal which is not taught in the classroom, whether they live in college dormitories, in rented rooms, or at home. Change in any number of human dimensions will take place during these years whether anyone provides for it or not, and whether the college gives it formal recognition or not. Perhaps the more significant question is whether, during these learning years, there is to be any useful correlation between intellectual growth and personal growth—that is, growth that includes all of the dimensions of the person. Is there to be any connection—indeed, any integrity—between intellectual maturing and emotional maturing, between culture and character? It is precisely this kind of integration of life to which both the smallness and the residential character of the college are intended to contribute.

In spite of occasional protests to the contrary, I believe

that many—perhaps most—students come to college with
the eager hope of finding precisely this kind of life integration. Surely President Perkins, of Cornell University,
is right:

> Hardly a student passes through our schools and colleges
> who hasn't his unique expectations for self-dicovery and
> fulfillment. These expectations may not always coincide
> with programs designed to meet social needs or with
> activities organized by a faculty in pursuit of the truth.
> . . . But these individual aspirations must be met, or our
> academic society will become as dehumanized and im-
> personal as our worst fears portend. And these aspira-
> tions must be met not simply by a curriculum that
> contains subject matter on students' minds, nor even by
> research that teachers and professors may sometimes
> share with their students. Nothing short of redesigning
> the environment of the academy itself will begin to
> answer the needs of students who must learn the difficult
> business of becoming effective adults.[11]

If the multiversity like Cornell must be prepared to re-
design its environment to bring about this broadened context for learning, the smaller college may have to engage
in its own kind of redesigning. Smallness and residentiality do not of themselves guarantee a desirable educational result for young men and women on their way to
becoming adults. So in our concern for the total personal
development of each student, we need to put some hard
questions on our agenda:

When does individual attention become a kind of institutional hovering which the student may find understand-
ably oppressive?

How can we prevent the sometimes subtle transition
from concern to meddling?

How can sympathetic and supportive relationships be maintained without turning the college into a pseudo-therapeutic institution?

How can the individual visibility which goes with small-ness be kept from discouraging genuine individuality?

How can residentiality provide for the privacy every growing person needs to sort himself out?

And how can we avoid the temptation to claim for certain forms of behavior the sanction of eternal wisdom when they are, in fact, only matters of prudence or taste?

IV

Second, institutional commitment. There are at least three reasons why we have sometimes lost our nerve at the point of a distinctive institutional posture in the educational world. One is fear that commitment may be inimical to academic effectiveness and integrity. Second is concern lest commitment be divisive within the college community. And third is a simple desire to avoid the agony and des-perately hard work that go with any carefully thought out and worked through consensus on principle, whether edu-cational or any other. Then perhaps we can best approach this issue of commitment by trying to see what happens to an institution when it is absent. Recently one of our most reputable Protestant colleges took a long and hard look at itself, and when the examination was over, the faculty member who directed the self-study wrote this:

> In a more personal judgment, I would venture to say that our greatest weakness lies in our failure to perceive any clear and compelling sense of purpose and direction in our undertaking as a college which could unify the faculty, the students, and the administration and the

many excellent programs [we sponsor]. . . . This lack
of purpose and direction is evidenced by the widespread
indifference to and lack of identification with the college
on the part of students, and . . . of faculty members as
well. It is present in the paradoxical statements [made
by many members of the college] that we do a good job
at helping students achieve a liberal education, . . . and
yet . . . the campus is intellectually dull and unexciting.
Surely something can be done about this situation in
which we have many excellent and successful parts but
in which the whole is somehow listless and disappointing.

I suspect that confession may bespeak the condition of
more than one college among us, and the earnest hope that
"surely something can be done" to change the listlessness
and disappointment will bespeak a hope that many of our
colleagues share. What that something may be is suggested by another person who participated in that same
self-study. He wrote:

There is danger in becoming so prescriptive that an institution becomes a mere propagandizer, and no longer
an institution engaged in the task of inquiry. Yet the
opposite has its limitations too. How "open" can a college be without becoming aimless and sterile? . . . It
seems to me that an institution would have a difficult
time promoting a general "sense of commitment" [in its
students] if by its institutional actions it did not demonstrate a commitment to something more specific than
"a sense of commitment." If it is imperative for an
institution of learning to be examining every phase of
life and thought, and thus even re-examining periodically
the aims and values which prompt their decisions, it is

equally imperative that it clarify and present openly the aims and values to which it is currently committed.

Berkeley educational researcher Warren Martin would agree. "Our problem," he has recently written,

> is that most schools have not been places characterized by conscious effort in this area. . . . Consequently, the educational philosophy is often determined willy-nilly, by the pressure of external circumstances or disciplinary biases, by hoary tradition or anticipatory opportunism. . . . On other campuses nothing is definite, so nothing is definitive. Where there is no philosophical framework, faculty and students lack an institutional standard against which to test themselves; and this is a day when faculty need such a standard because they are at the stage of life when, as Erik Erikson put it, the issue is integrity, just as students need it because they are at the stage in life where, as Edgar Friedenberg has shown, the issue is self-identity. And neither faculty nor students can decide such issues in a void.[12]

If Martin's research findings are correct, as the experience of the two men involved in the self-study seems to confirm, then instead of compromising academic effectiveness and integrity, institutional commitment is precisely one of the necessary conditions for such effectiveness and integrity. Rather than being divisive, it provides a unifying sense of direction and purpose as important to those who may not sympathize with it as to those who do. And if such commitment comes only out of agonizing process, that agony may be preferable to a dispiriting and demoralizing normlessness.

V

Third, liberal education. What is at stake in maintaining the liberal character of our educational programs is our intention to be institutions of humane learning. Or to put the matter negatively, to the degree that we lose our liberal character, to that degree we shall reduce the possibilities for humanization in the educational experience. If the Protestant college has had a single hallmark, surely it has been a determination to direct all of its educational resources toward enhancing the human. This is why we have been concerned to design an environment for learning marked both by individuality and by community.

But the humane and humanizing concerns of a college cannot be adequately accomplished by counseling resources and supportive relationships, by responsible student self-government and imaginative social activities. The curriculum itself has an absolutely indispensable role to play in enhancing the human. To be a man is to have a world, and the shape of the man is measured by the dimensions of the world that is accessible to his reach. Humanness is crabbed and cramped wherever men and women are restricted in their capacity to experience; the limitations they see in the world, internalized, become the limits of the self. Humanness is expanded and enhanced wherever men and women have a widened capacity to experience and thus to internalize reality in its multiform richness.

Surely this is what is intended in the distinctive style of liberal arts teaching. A course in literature, for example, is not to be taught as if every student in the class were preparing to become a professional critic. It is, rather, to be taught in such a way that every student, regardless of his professional intent, may increase his competence as a sensitive, informed, discerning, critical reader of literature. And what is true of literature is true of the other disciplines as well. They are to be considered as forms of experience to be entered into, rather than as crafts to be reproduced.

And when we design a curriculum that permits students entrance into a wide variety of universes of discourse, surely that is because we believe that no single method of approaching our human experience is sufficient in dealing with the full range and richness of reality. For all its astonishing usefulness, the method of the natural sciences needs to be supplemented and complemented by the study of history and the peculiar perceptiveness of the artist; and the arts, in their turn, need to be complemented and supplemented by the vision of the scientist. When the student is asked to distribute his courses among the several divisions of the curriculum, it is with the hope that he will thus come to understand these distinctive avenues into experience, in order to expand his intellectual appreciation of them, and *in order to expand his power to experience*.

If we are to modify our liberal tradition in learning, let it be because we have found some better way to enhance the human.

VI

Fourth, concern for the meaning of experience. Here I want to make a very practical, perhaps even controversial, proposal. To put it directly, I believe that the Protestant college must determine to give a priority to the arts and the humanities that will assure them a place in the curriculum which matches the importance of any other area of study, and which insists that the quality of instruction in these disciplines be unsurpassed in the college.

It is the peculiar function of the arts and the humanities to probe the questions of the meaning of life, both personal and social. Their ends have to do not so much with information as with outlooks, not so much with dispassionate facts as with the passions facts are made to serve. It is the peculiar mission of the arts and the humanities to make us aware of the meanings men serve, often unwittingly and therefore dangerously, and to dare to propose new perspectives around which to order our practical activities.

There is no doubt in my mind that the natural sciences will continue to enjoy prestige and priority in our national purposes generally and in our educational institutions particularly. Neither is there any doubt that the social sciences will become the beneficiaries of a sharply rising prestige in the immediate future. One could see this coming long before the events of July, 1967, but those events were as good as a guarantee. Before that July, it was widely believed that with the end of the Vietnam war, education would stand highest on the national list of unfinished business, with massive federal support to be expected from an education-conscious Congress. Since the riots of 1967 and their aftermath, that prediction is less confident in view of the urgency of our urban problems. Now it appears that the American city may come to lead the list of national unfinished business. This clearly portends an increasing awareness of and support for the social sciences, since only with a strategy informed by the best work of its scholars do the problems of the city even begin to appear corrigible.

And where will all this leave the arts and the humanities —the visual and dramatic arts, music, literature, philosophy, religion, history? In terms of their place within our national goals—and, I fear as a consequence, in our educational goals as well—it will leave them running a poor third, with little attention and even less investment left over from the sciences. Yet surely it takes nothing away from the sciences—nothing, at least, to which they have any legitimate intellectual claim—to insist that the arts and the humanities have a role to play which is equally critical, though admittedly more subtle, in determining not only the survival of the nation but the character of the nation that survives. It is their function, as I have already said— through imagination and reflection, poetry and philosophy —to clarify and illuminate, to expose and explore and test the values that are resident within the practical alternatives which confront us. To permit that illumination to dim, even by so much as a few candlepower, is not in the national interest.

You may be prepared to agree with all this without seeing why I charge the Protestant college with special responsibility in the matter. I do so, for one thing, precisely because it is a *Protestant* college, precisely because proportionate support for the arts and the humanities is one of the ways in which we can make good on our claim to serve a distinctively religious purpose with academic freedom and integrity.

Religion is only secondarily a matter of ritual observance and moral code, of theological creeds and of churches. Primarily, religion is a matter of our meanings. Ritual and code, creed and church, are only the servants, the tangible expressions of the meanings that matter most to us. And there is no single source, even within the Christian religion, from which these meanings are derived. If the Biblical tradition is our primary source, with Jesus Christ at its center, it is by no means our only source. Indeed, the Biblical tradition itself constantly points beyond itself. Israel's prophets acknowledged God's revealing activity in the lives of other nations; Paul declared himself to be debtor both to Jews and to Greeks. And if the center of our faith is not simply Jesus but Jesus Christ—not simply a man trapped within the limitations of his own history but the creative Word that God speaks throughout his creation—then the Christian will have to be attentive to what God may have to say to him through the general culture and history, regardless of how apparently lacking those may be in credentials for such communication.

All of which is to say that the Protestant college has a distinctive stake in keeping alive and lively those academic disciplines whose unique function it is to probe the meanings of life, not forcing those disciplines into some premature or dishonest endorsement of a presumably Christian view of things, but leaving them free to be faithful in response to the Creative Spirit, believing that to be their best contribution to our own Christian faithfulness.

My second reason for assigning special responsibility to the Protestant college for support of the arts and the humanities is a purely pragmatic one. The Protestant college is, as I have said, typically a small college. It cannot command the resources and should not attempt to reproduce the specialized technical efforts of the comprehensive universities. It should, rather, do what it can do excellently within its own scope and reach. Increasingly in these days, advanced work in the natural sciences requires sophisticated equipment which the small college cannot hope to possess, and even in the social sciences advanced study and research are more and more tied to technical hardware which few small schools can command. This does not mean that we should cease to teach the natural and social sciences, or that we should not teach them at the very highest level of competence of which we are capable.

Nor does it mean that we need to be defensive about our preparation of scientific scholars, since we believe that technical competence is the more effective when it is set in a broad historical and cultural base which the more specialized schools, with all their hardware, do not provide. But it may mean that we shall have to recognize certain kinds of limitations in our teaching of the sciences.

We should also recognize that the arts and the humanities have quite different requirements. They need sophisticated library holdings rather than complicated machinery. They need space and time rather than gadgets. And above all, they need a climate of encouragement which recognizes the importance of their noetic and synoptic work.

There is absolutely no reason why the Protestant college cannot take the academic leadership for the future in the arts and the humanities, no reason why it cannot provide the best teaching in these fields to be found anywhere in America. If it does so, it will become the patron and transmitter of a vital heritage that is seriously in danger of being ignored if not disadvantaged, to the peril of all. It could find the means to do so. It lacks only the will.

VII

Fifth, moral seriousness. It is commonplace to observe that our American culture is experiencing a period of moral crisis and confusion which is more serious than any in recent history. On the one hand, it is clear that a large part of our society is suffering a loss of moral nerve not, I fear, unlike that moral dullness which came upon the German people in the thirties and perhaps for a similar reason: we are being accustomed to brutalism, whether in the primitive villages of Vietnam or on the streets of Detroit. On the other hand, there is a minority, not to be identified with any single social or racial group, that is aggressively nihilistic. For these native American nihilists there are no objective ethical standards, there are only friends and enemies.

And there is at least one other group made up of those who are morally troubled, who are actively searching, not as a means of delay or escape, but as a means of finding a place to stand. Although all three groups are found throughout the community, I think this third group is probably to be found in greater numbers on the American college campus than anywhere else.

I fully expect that this moral crisis will be with us for some time to come, and that means that our colleges have some hard decisions to make. In some places, it may be possible to control moral unrest either by subtle academic and disciplinary pressures or by outright heavy-handed administrative suppression, though that will be tragic, if not immoral, when it happens. In other places, it may be possible to upstage moral unrest by creating magnificent distractions, though that will be a frightful waste. In some places at least, it may be hoped, moral crisis will be taken as a constructive occasion for moral learning.

Even if there were no crisis, the liberal arts college generally, and the Protestant college in particular, could not escape the obligation to concern itself with moral learning. Knowledge, as we have increasing reason to know, is power, and any power unrestrained by moral sensibilities is a dangerous and capricious instrument. Moral learning is of concern to the liberal arts because, apart from an explicit moral sense, the supposedly cultured man can serve inhumane ends as readily as humane ones. Literary critic

George Steiner has recently written, "We know now that a man can read Goethe or Rilke in the evening, that he can play Bach or Schubert, and go to his day's work at Auschwitz in the morning." [13]

And there is a distinctively Christian dimension in all this. The Biblical faith insists that those who know the truth must do more than tell the truth: they must also *do the truth*. Knowing the truth always imposes the obligation to moral seriousness: it is not enough to know the truth without doing something about it. Harry Emerson Fosdick once said that when the rich young ruler consulted Jesus, he came in with a theoretical problem on his mind— but he went out with a moral problem on his hands! That ought to define the result of Christian higher education.

There is, I think, a distinctive and legitimate role in moral learning to be played by the academic classroom. One of the things that feed moral crisis is the absence of clarity about moral implications and alternatives. Moral conviction can grow in us only when we see the possibilities clearly enough that they become live options for acceptance or rejection. In our teaching, the more we can sharpen the ethical issues, the more chance there is that we shall contribute to the growth of moral conviction. How one can teach the twentieth-century novel, or urban sociology, or genetics, or ancient history, without exposing its specific ethical content and implication is beyond me. Yet I fear that it is done regularly and with the blithe confidence that the subject has been treated with academic adequacy. I want to enter a vigorous dissent from that kind of teaching and to insist that it fails to take seriously either the subject to be learned or the educational need of the learner. Moral learning in the classroom need be neither special pleading nor academic prostitution, but only a recognition of the pervasiveness of the ethical in every human activity.

Two articles in an issue of *Saturday Review* have struck me forcibly with their implications for the moral seriousness that must attend our academic study. Kalamazoo Professor Richard Means provocatively suggests that

> our contemporary moral crisis . . . goes much deeper than questions of political power and law, of urban riots and slums. It may, at least in part, reflect American society's almost utter disregard for the value of nature.[14]

Professor Means makes an impressive case for the possibility that when man exploits the natural world unfeelingly, thus destroying his capacity to wonder at it and to enter into its awesome mystery, he demeans and diminishes his own humanity and thus loses a part of his capacity to deal humanly with other men.

In the same issue, Rockefeller University Professor René Dubos writes:

> Ignorance of science should be no excuse in technicized societies because all important decisions now have scientific determinants. This does not mean that everyone should be a science graduate. . . . But it does mean that responsible citizens should acquire the kind of general understanding that facilitates recognition and evaluation of the social consequences of science and technology. For lack of this understanding, the citizen will have to submit to the tyranny of the expert who will then become a decision-maker without being answerable to the community. In contrast, if the public can share in a more enlightened manner in the decision-making process involving scientific problems, democratic societies may regain the social coherence which is the condition of their survival.[15]

Both Professor Means and Professor Dubos are raising a question about the morality of knowledge which ought to force a reexamination of the way in which science is taught in the liberal arts college, for the general student as well as for the specialist. Do our present courses and teaching methods—especially the typical requirement of one year of laboratory science—in fact contribute to that valuing of the natural world which also enhances the human and thus sustains the moral? Do they create the kind of scientific understanding that permits intelligent participation in shaping a rational social policy with respect to science and technology? If not, then they exacerbate the moral problem. There is no morally neutral ground in the science classroom, nor is there, indeed, in any other classroom.

But moral learning is more than learning about morals, important as that is. It is possible for a student to cheat on an examination in philosophical ethics without ever glimpsing the irony. College life outside the classroom has its own contribution to make toward a growing clarity of moral conviction.

First, the college should provide a platform for forthright advocates of a wide variety of points of view as a contribution to an informed understanding of the conflict of ideas in our time.

Second, those who administer and teach must be prepared to come clean on the issue by making their own moral commitments visible. No one is born with convictions; a student will learn what it is to hold a conviction in the presence of convictional persons. It ought to distress us more than it does that the most visible convictional persons in our time are at the psychopathic fringe, not at the academic center!

Third, there should exist on the campus the widest possible freedom for trying out convictions which is consistent with a proper environment for study, an appropriate concern for the rights of others, and a due regard for law.

And finally, the college ought to find ways to make use of its peculiar freedom as a private institution to do what public institutions are not free to do: to affirm the historical wisdom that moral change is not necessarily moral progress; to affirm that, contrary to popular opinion, goodness is not out of fashion; and to affirm its conviction that the source of human good is to be found in Jesus Christ.

VIII

Sixth, the academic study of religion. I take it that the Protestant college has the responsibility to increase, among Christians and non-Christians alike, an intelligent understanding and appreciation of the Christian tradition in its literary, ethical, institutional, and intellectual forms. The most incredible misinformation can be found among supposedly educated men and women concerning even the most basic facts of the Christian tradition. One place, therefore, where the educational and religious missions of the college converge is in the concern to create a more religiously literate public.

That a Protestant college should possess superior resources and competence in the academic study of religion seems to me axiomatic. That such instruction has, in too many instances, been anything but superior is admittedly an impressionistic judgment but one that I am unable to fault. In some Protestant colleges, enrollment in religion courses is artificially inflated and gives a false sense of the vitality of religious instruction. Students are too often found in religion classrooms, not because they have been drawn there by the superior quality of the learning experience, but solely because it is a graduation requirement. I am not, for the moment, questioning the validity of required religion courses, but I am deploring the possibility that such requirements may provide a safe haven for dull, sometimes uninformed, inferior instruction. If we needed any evidence for the generally undistinguished level of academic religion in the Protestant college, it could be found in the fact that scholarly leadership in the field has not, unhappily, come from such schools. In an earlier time it came from the graduate theological seminaries, but it seems now ironically to be shifting to state-supported institutions.

There is a sense in which the reputation of the college as a Protestant Christian institution—at least among its own teachers and students—will hinge directly upon the academic reputation of its religion department, and I would argue that this is precisely as it should be. If the department cannot win full respect as an academic department, there is no reason why the college should be taken seriously as a *Christian college,* since it fails to treat its own professed tradition with sufficient intellectual respect. Piety and good intentions may be admirable in a church, but they are no substitute for scholarship in a college religion department. Religious scholarship in the Protestant college ought to be good enough to provide the bench mark by which other disciplines measure their own competence, and nothing short of that should satisfy us.

IX

Finally on this agenda is the tradition of humane service. Here, as in the case of moral seriousness, I have come increasingly to believe that we too often ignore the legitimate and even essential role the academic classroom has to play. We quite plausibly assume that motivating students toward humanitarian effort is a matter of inviting the right chapel speakers and of channeling extracurricular activities in constructive directions. And when the humanitarianism these awaken is disappointing, we wonder why. Part of the answer, I think, is that there is so little real humanity at the heart of the educational experience, the classroom.

Simply consider how the student himself is commonly excluded from the classroom as an existing human being. He is welcomed as a detached intellect but too seldom acknowledged as a man. I suspect that Binx Bolling, the central character in Walker Percy's novel *The Moviegoer,* has told us pretty clearly what much of our classroom learning is like:

> Until recent years, I read only "fundamental" books, that is, key books on key subjects, such as *War and Peace,* the novel of novels; *A Study of History,* the solution of the problem of time; Schroedinger's *What is Life?,* Einstein's *The Universe as I See It,* and such. During those years I stood outside the universe and sought to understand it. I lived in my room as an Anyone living Anywhere and read fundamental books and only for diversion took walks around the neighborhood and saw an occasional movie. Certainly it did not matter to me where I was when I read such a book as *The Expanding Universe.* The greatest success of this enterprise, which I call my vertical search, came one night when I sat in a hotel room in Birmingham and read a book called *The Chemistry of Life.* When I finished it, it seemed to me that the main goals of my search were reached or were in principle reachable, whereupon I went out and saw a

movie called "It Happened One Night," which was itself very good. A memorable night. The only difficulty was that though the universe had been disposed of, I myself was left over. There I lay in my hotel room with my search over yet still obliged to draw one breath and then the next.[16]

And if the learner is too seldom acknowledged as a man, there may be precious little of humanity in what he is taught. Professor William Muehl, of Yale, has recently written something that strikes me as a particularly telling parable of our academic unreality. "Some time ago," says Professor Muehl,

I saw a painting which was entitled "The Brokenness of Man." It was a splendidly abstract thing, a complex of lights, shadows, jagged angles, and broken lines. I wanted to stand and look at it for a long time, take it home and hang it on my wall and invite my friends in to see it while we sipped coffee and nibbled crackers and cheese. I contemplated the deep discussions which it might stimulate and heard myself saying often that it really takes an artist to catch the truth about things.

But then I remembered a photograph that I had seen shortly before. It had been taken by Weegee, the camera-man who specialized in recording the seamy side of New York City. And it showed a drunk lying unconscious in a Harlem doorway. He had a three-day growth of beard on his face, a shock of unkempt hair, vomit all over his chest, snot running from his nose, a bottle clutched in the crook of his elbow. This was a broken man. And I did not linger in front of that portrait. Nor did I long to take it home and hang it on my wall and have my friends in to look at it as we sipped coffee and

nibbled crackers and cheese. This was a broken man.
And all I wanted was to get away from him as rapidly
as possible.[17]

Am I suggesting that when—in art and history and literature and psychology and sociology and biology and economics and philosophy—when in these disciplines we
examine the brokenness of man, such a creature as this
should be present in the classroom? I am suggesting that
if ways cannot be found literally or figuratively to get him
in, then the classroom should be moved where he is.

Chancellor Caldwell, of North Carolina State, has put
the case pointedly for ending our educational "gamesman-
ship" by making the real world our classroom. He writes:

Could it be that [what we need] . . . is a fresh, no-holds-
barred, nothing-sacred, scrutiny of the whole form and
process of what we call collegiate education? Could it
just be that we need to read Whitehead and Dewey again
not just for what they mean for elementary and secondary
education but for their meaning to us in higher education and our influence on the lower grades? Could it
just be that our curriculum should be rebuilt extensively
around problems of the human condition and of mankind's destiny? Could it just be that our competitive
striving for ill-defined academic standards and measures
of esteem in the world of scholarship have burdened us
with conventions and habits that crowd out the learning
that comes from caring and the caring that comes from
contact and insight?

Could it be that each of our standard discipline-framed
curricula of tool subjects and professional subjects and
values subjects and knowledge-acquisition subjects needs
a thorough overhaul? And should not this overhauling

make room for perhaps a quarter or one-third of the student's time from freshman through senior years to be devoted to problem-oriented involvement, loaded, as Whitehead would say, with "first-handedness"? . . .

As deeply as I believe in the virtues of knowledge and learning, in the virtues of the informed intellect, and the present desirability of a college degree in the marketplace, I am convinced even more that the students who have chosen to serve in the Peace Corps and in Vista have chosen a sure way to educate themselves into the contemporary world. Whatever in their college experience may have caused them to apply and make the commitment needs to be better understood by the educators and taken as a clue to the reform of higher education.[18]

This, then, is an agenda worthy of the Protestant college in the 1970's. These are the things that I think we ought to be about. They are the things we have always said we intended to do. This is time not for a failure of nerve but for a recovery of that self-respect which will free us to do them.

Notes

As indicated in the Foreword and acknowledgments, some of the essays in this volume are abridgments of longer works. The editors believe that it would only confuse our readers if the original note numbers were unvaryingly retained. Since in some instances sections omitted in abridgment also omit quotations and their accompanying note numbers, retention of the numbers used in the original essays would leave occasional gaps in the numerical sequence. The editors have therefore taken the liberty of renumbering notes where necessary, in order to maintain numerical sequence and clarity throughout the abridgments. It should also be noted that only notes required by direct citations in the essays have been retained; notes that expand the discussion or provide examples have been omitted because of space limitations here.

CHAPTER 1. Objectivity vs. Commitment, *by Huston Smith*

1. H. A. Hodges, *Objectivity and Impartiality* (London: SCM Press, Ltd., 1946), pp. 12–17.

CHAPTER 2. Institutional Commitment: A Social Scientist's View, *by Harry R. Davis*

1. Charles Perrow, "Organizational Goals," in *International Encyclopedia of the Social Sciences*, Vol. 11, p. 305.
2. Philip Selznick, *Leadership in Administration* (Row, Peterson & Company, 1957), p. 5.

3. *Ibid.*, pp. 7 f.

4. *Ibid.*, pp. 5 f.

5. Talcott Parsons, *Structure and Process in Modern Societies* (The Free Press of Glencoe, 1960), p. 17.

6. Selznick, *op. cit.*, p. 17.

7. *Ibid.*, pp. 19, 22, 35, and 40.

8. Louis Schneider, "Institution," in Julius Gould and William Kolb, eds., *A Dictionary of the Social Sciences* (The Free Press of Glencoe, 1964), p. 338.

9. *Ibid.*

10. Nevitt Sanford, ed., *College and Character* (John Wiley & Sons, Inc., 1964), p. 14.

11. Philip Jacob, *Changing Values in College* (Harper & Brothers, 1957), Ch. 6.

12. Morris Keeton and Conrad Hilberry, from a mimeographed manuscript entitled "The Future of Liberal Arts Colleges," subsequently incorporated in *Struggle and Promise: A Future for Colleges* (McGraw-Hill Book Company, Inc., 1969).

13. Kenneth Hansen, *Philosophy for American Education* (Prentice-Hall, Inc., 1960), pp. 132 f.

14. Sanford, *op. cit.*, p. 298.

CHAPTER 3. The Sectarian Nature of Liberal Education,
                    by Lloyd J. Averill

1. John Sloan Dickey, "Conscience and the Undergraduate," *Atlantic Monthly*, April, 1955, p. 33.

2. George Stern, "Higher Education in the Mass Society," *Current Issues in Higher Education 1964* (Association for Higher Education, 1964), p. 115.

3. Lloyd J. Averill, *A Strategy for the Protestant College* (The Westminster Press, 1966), pp. 14–16.

4. Gerhard Spiegler, from an unpublished paper, "Theology as a Discipline in the University."

5. E. J. Shoben, "The Liberal Arts: A Modern Concept?"

AGB Reports (Association of Governing Boards, November–December, 1967), p. 5.

6. Fred Newmann and Donald Oliver, "Education and Community," *Harvard Educational Review*, Winter, 1967, p. 61.

7. Erlend Jacobsen, "Goddard College," *The Christian Scholar*, Summer, 1967, p. 91.

8. Arthur Borden, "New College," *ibid.*, pp. 97 and 99.

9. Spiegler, *op. cit.*

10. Newmann and Oliver, *loc. cit.*, p. 61.

11. *Ibid.*, pp. 61–62 (emphasis added).

12. *Ibid.*, p. 62.

CHAPTER 4. The Identity of the Christian College,
     by William W. Jellema

1. René Dubos, *So Human an Animal* (Charles Scribner's Sons, 1968), pp. 161 f.

2. Kenneth Keniston, "Faces in the Lecture Room," *Yale Alumni Magazine*, April, 1966, pp. 32, 33, and 28.

3. Kenneth Underwood, in William Kolb, *New Wine* (St. Louis, 1969), p. 18. *New Wine* is a summary and interpretation of *The Church, The University, and Social Policy* by Kenneth Underwood (Wesleyan University Press, 1969).

4. W. H. Cowley, "The Role of Anthropocentrism," *Liberal Education*, March, 1960, p. 46.

5. Nathan Pusey, cited in *The Christian Century*, October 14, 1953, p. 1159.

6. Kolb, *op. cit.*, p. 64.

7. Walter Moberly, *The Crisis in the University* (London: Macmillan & Co., Ltd., 1949), p. 295.

8. Keniston, *loc. cit.*, p. 33.

CHAPTER 6. Natural Order and Transcendent Order,
     by William G. Pollard

1. Robert Oppenheimer, *Science and the Common Understanding* (Simon & Schuster, Inc., 1953), p. 93.

CHAPTER 9. Academic Excellence and Moral Value,
     by William W. Jellema

1. Louis T. Benezet, "The Trouble with Excellence," in Paul Woodring and John Scanlon, eds., *American Education Today* (McGraw-Hill Book Company, Inc., 1963), pp. 7 and 12.
2. William L. Shirer, *The Rise and Fall of the Third Reich* (Simon & Schuster, Inc., 1960), p. 787.
3. Sydney D. Bailey, "Conversation in Pingshan," *The Christian Century*, June 11, 1958, pp. 693 f.
4. Benezet, *loc. cit.,* p. 13.
5. Cited by Robert S. Morison, in "The Need for New Types of Excellence," *Daedalus*, Vol. 90, No. 4 (Fall, 1961), p. 776.
6. Meg Greenfield, "The Great American Morality Play," *The Reporter*, June 8, 1961, p. 15.
7. Kenneth Keniston, "Social Change and Youth in America," *Daedalus*, Vol. 91, No. 1 (Winter, 1962), pp. 148 ff. *et passim*.
8. Morison, *loc. cit.,* p. 774.
9. Martin Mayer, "Twice Progressive," a review of *The Transformation of the School* by Lawrence A. Cremin, in *The Reporter*, June 8, 1961, p. 39.
10. Cited by Geoffrey Barraclough, "Waiting for Hitler," a review of *The Early Goebbels Diaries*, in *Manchester Guardian Weekly*, August 16, 1962, p. 11.

CHAPTER 10. Biblical Realism as a Norm, *by Will Herberg*

1. Dwight M. Donaldson, *Studies in Muslim Ethics* (London: Society for Promoting Christian Knowledge, 1953), p. 109.

2. Hajo Holborn, "Greek and Modern Concepts of History," *Journal of the History of Ideas*, Vol. X, No. 1 (January, 1949).

CHAPTER 11. Christian Ethical Community as a Norm, *by Waldo Beach*

1. Robert Hutchins, *Education for Freedom* (Louisiana State University Press, 1943), p. 26.
2. Kenneth Boulding, *The Organizational Revolution* (Harper & Brothers, 1953), p. 63.
3. Harvard Committee, *General Education in a Free Society* (Harvard University Press, 1945), p. 39.
4. H. Richard Niebuhr *et al., The Purpose of the Church and Its Ministry* (Harper & Brothers, 1956), p. 37.

CHAPTER 12. A Pluralistic Model, *by Warren B. Martin*

1. Talcott Parsons, "The Problem of the Theory of Change," in W. G. Bennis, K. D. Berne, and R. Chinn, eds., *The Planning of Change* (Holt, Rinehart & Winston, Inc., 1961), p. 215.
2. William James, *Pragmatism* (Longmans, Green & Company, 1928), pp. 49–50.
3. Cf. Viktor Frankl, *The Doctor and the Soul* (Alfred A. Knopf, Inc., 1960), p. *x*.
4. Martin Buber, *Between Man and Man* (Beacon Press, Inc., 1955), p. 96.
5. Clark Kerr, *Center Diary* (Center for the Study of Democratic Institutions, October–November, 1966), p. 11.
6. Roger Heyns, in an address, "The Nature of the Academic Community," before the American Council on Education, New Orleans, October 13, 1966.

CHAPTER 13. A Singular Model, *by Lloyd J. Averill*

1. Warren B. Martin, "Stalkers of Meaning," *The Journal of Higher Education*, October, 1967, p. 372.

2. Quoted in Walter Adams and Adrian Jaffe, "Government and the Universities: A Crisis in Identity," *The Progressive*, January, 1968, p. 28.

3. *Ibid.*

4. Paul Miller, *The Professional School and World Affairs* (Education and World Affairs, September, 1967).

5. Martin, *loc. cit.,* pp. 364–365.

6. Quoted in Earl J. McGrath, *The Liberal Arts College and the Emergent Caste System* (Teachers College Press, 1966), pp. 38–39.

7. *Ibid.,* pp. 42–43.

8. Herbert Stroup, *Freedom and Responsibility in Higher Education* (Christian Faith and Higher Education Institute), p. 16.

9. R. E. Gruen, *Our Graduates Speak Out* (Office of the Dean of Students, Brooklyn College, 1967), pp. 12–13.

10. John Caldwell, *Bulletin on International Education* (American Council on Education, December 15, 1967).

11. James A. Perkins, *The University and Due Process* (American Council on Education, 1967), p. 10.

12. Martin, *loc. cit.,* p. 365.

13. George Steiner, *Language and Silence: Essays on Language, Literature, and the Inhuman* (Atheneum Publishers, 1967).

14. Richard Means, "Why Worry About Nature?", *Saturday Review*, December 2, 1967, p. 71.

15. René Dubos, "Scientists Alone Can't Do the Job," *ibid.*

16. Walker Percy, *The Moviegoer* (Alfred A. Knopf, Inc., 1961), pp. 69–70.

17. William Muehl, from an unpublished sermon, "The Reality of God."

18. Caldwell, *op. cit.*